Contents

Proprietary terms

Credits and acknowledgements

Editors **Neil and Roswitha Morris**
Cartoons by **Claire Bretécher**

Introduction

Anyone learning a foreign language wants to be able to speak it as it is really spoken. This book will help you achieve this. Most coursebooks tend to reflect "standard" language—the language you hear on the radio or television or in formal contexts. This book covers the language of everyday, informal social situations.

A text written only in "spoken language" looks odd. Situations which are perfectly clear in conversation are not so easy to understand when reduced to dialogues on a page. Tapes and videos require special equipment. Cartoon strips overcome these difficulties and are an ideal vehicle for the efficient learning of spoken language. The characters feel real and their roles are very clear. The situations are immediately accessible and do not need to be described at length. Added to which, in Germany cartoons are extremely popular and enjoyed by adults and teenagers alike. Claire Bretécher's cartoons are no exception; they are well known and loved.

Spoken language is different from standard language for several reasons. It uses words which rarely appear in written form except in dictionaries (e.g. **Balg** instead of **Kind**). Some grammatical rules which are strictly applied when writing are often ignored when speaking. Abbreviated forms of words are used more freely (e.g. **wie gehts dir** instead of **wie geht es dir**).

The German texts have been written to be suitable for learners, and each one introduces a theme developed in the material which accompanies each story. A more detailed description of all the sections of the book is given in **How to use the book**.

The stories help learners to memorize themes and new words, and vocabulary learning becomes an enjoyable and rewarding experience.

How to use the book

This book is designed to make vocabulary learning both efficient and enjoyable. It is built around thirty cartoon strips and themes, each presented on a double-page spread, with a clear emphasis on spoken language.

Each story is supplemented by three sections:

1. Understanding the text
This lists all the key words used in the cartoon strip on the facing page and gives grammatical information as well as contextual translations.

2. Key Structures
This section lists and explains phrases which are hard to understand even if all the individual constituents are known. It also supplies information on those phrases commonly used in spoken language that will be useful for a learner.

3. Vocabulary
This section groups together the essential words and phrases from the vocabulary-building topic introduced in the story. Grammatical information such as noun genders is also supplied.

Additional notes in text bubbles explain culture-specific references appearing in the text.

For easy access, the topics are listed in the table of **contents**.

The **glossary** at the end of the book lists all the words that appear in the stories and vocabulary sections and their translations with the relevant page number(s). Informal words used only in spoken language are clearly marked with the symbol ◉.

Advice on pronunciation rules and sounds in German is given in the **Guide to pronunciation**.

List of abbreviations

adj	adjective
adv	adverb
art	article
conj	conjunction
interj	interjection
nf	feminine noun
nm	masculine noun
nm/f	masculine/feminine noun
nn	neuter noun
pl	plural
prep	preposition
pron	pronoun
v	verb
v sep	separable verb
*	irregular verb
◉	WARNING: this symbol indicates that a word is used only in spoken language
→	see

Guide to pronunciation

The following are general guidelines to the way in which German is pronounced.

Vowel sounds

German vowels are pure sounds, whereas in English vowels usually have one sound quickly followed by another. This applies to vowel sounds written with two letters — **au**, **ei**, etc. — which also have a single sound.

In German, each vowel has a long and a short form: for example, an **a** can be long, as in **Bahn**, or short, as in **hat**. As a general rule, vowels are long when followed by **h** (**Jahr**) or by one consonant (**war**) and short when followed by two consonants (**lassen**).

When they follow consonants, vowels are not normally run on as they are in English. For example, **ein Apfel** is pronounced as two separate words, whereas an apple might be run together as if it were one word, 'anapple'.

Particular care must be taken with the umlaut sounds — **ä**, **ö** and **ü** — which do not exist in English.

German vowel	long or short	German example	nearest English equivalent
a	short	hat	vowel sound between hat and hut
a	long	Jahr	far
ä	short	Geschäft	left
ä	long	Käse	between pair and pace
ai	long	Mai	my
au	long	auf	cow
äu	long	Mäuse	boy
e	short	Essen	lesson
e	long	geben	gate
e	short, in unstressed syllables	Name	ago
ei	long	weit	right
eu	long	Zeug	boy
i	short	bist	bit
i	long	ihn	ease
ie	long	viel	feel
o	short	Post	lost
o	long	Ton	bone (pronounced without moving tongue or lips)
ö	short	können	cur (with short u)
ö	long	böse	burn (with long u)
u	short	null	put
u	long	gut	moon
ü	short, like the French tu	küssen	round your lips and try to say ee
ü	long, like the French tu	über	round your lips and try to say longer ee
y	long, like the French tu	Typ	round your lips and try to say longer ee

Consonants

Some German consonants change pronunciation according to their position in a word. For example, at the end of a word or syllable, b, d and g are pronounced p, t and k respectively.

German consonant	notes	German example	nearest English equivalent
b	at the beginning of a word	Bank	bank
b	at the end of a word or syllable	ab	up
c	hard, before a, o, u	Café	café
c	soft, before e, i	Cembalo	chew
ch	after a, o, u	acht	loch, pronounced in the Scottish way
ch	after e, i	ich	similar to the first sound in huge
ch	hard	Mechaniker	car
chs		sechs	six
d	at the beginning of a word	dann	done
d	at the end of a word or syllable	Rad	dart
dt		Stadt	cat
f		Fuß	fat
g	at the beginning of a word	Gast	guest
g	at the end of a word	Tag	park
g	–ig, at the end of a word	lustig	similar to the first sound in huge
h		hat	hat
h	at the end of a syllable	sah, sehen	not pronounced, and makes the previous vowel long
j		ja	yet
k		kann	kit
l		Leute	lot
m		Maus	mouse
n		Name	name
p		Paket	parcel
qu		Quatsch	pronounced kv (to make 'kvatsh')
r	rolled, usually at the back of the mouth	raten	rest
s	hissing ss sound	es	set
s	before a vowel, z sound	Hose	zoo
s	before p or t at the beginning of a syllable, sh sound	Stunde	ship
sch	like English sh	Schule	shut
ß	same as ss	heiß	press
t		toll	tip
tsch	like English ch	deutsch	chin
v	like English f	vier	fat
v	in most foreign words	Video	video
w	like English v	was	van
x		Taxi	taxi
z	like English ts	Zug	hits

WARUM ICH?

Understanding the text

anderer/andere/anderes (adj)	other
außer (prep)	except (for)
das Badezimmer –s,– (nn)	bathroom
dann (adv)	then
die (pron)	who
dieser/diese/dieses (adj)	this, (pl) these
dir (pron)	(to) you
du (pron)	you
eingeschlossen (v*)	→einschließen
einsam (adv)	lonely
einschließen (v sep*)	to lock in
es (pron)	it
die Frage –,–n (nf)	question
haben (v*)	to have
hast (v*)	→haben
hier (adv)	here
ich (pron)	I, me
das Ich –(s),–(s) (nn)	self

im = in dem (prep)	in
irgendwo (adv)	somewhere, anywhere
mein (adj)	my
mir (pron)	(to) me
mit (prep)	with
niemand (pron)	nobody
oder (conj)	or
rülps	burp
sich einsam fühlen	to feel lonely
sprechen (v*)	to talk, to speak
spricht (v*)	→sprechen
und (conj)	and
warum ich?	why me?
wenn (conj)	if
wenn es dich gibt	if you exist
wer (pron)	who
wo (adv)	where
das Zeichen –s,– (nn)	sign, signal
zuhören (v sep)	to listen
zuhört (v)	→zuhören

Describing People

my name is Anita	ich heiße Anita
my nickname is Fizz	Fizz ist mein Spitzname
surname	der Nachname
I'm sixteen	ich bin sechzehn
I am 1.68 m (tall)	ich bin 1,68 (groß)
I weigh 55 kilos	ich wiege 55 Kilo
my hair is blond	ich habe blonde Haare
his eyes are blue	er hat blaue Augen
her hair is long/curly	sie hat lange Haare/sie hat Locken
straight hair	glatte Haare
I prefer short hair	ich habe lieber kurze Haare
she's got a pony-tail	sie hat einen Pferdeschwanz
he is growing a beard	er lässt sich einen Bart wachsen
he shaved his moustache	er hat seinen Schnurrbart abrasiert
he wears glasses	er trägt eine Brille
I live near Munich	ich wohne in der Nähe von München
I live in a house/flat	ich wohne in einem Haus/in einer Wohnung
my room is on the first floor	mein Zimmer ist im ersten Stock
I live with my friends	ich wohne mit meinen Freunden zusammen
I live at home	ich wohne bei meinen Eltern
pleasant	nett
ambitious	ehrgeizig
funny	lustig
intelligent	intelligent
to be in a good mood	guter Laune sein, gute Laune haben
she is always in a good mood	sie hat immer gute Laune
to be in a bad mood	schlechter Laune sein, schlechte Laune haben
polite	höflich
lazy	faul
nice	sympathisch
tall	groß
fat	fett
thin	dünn
slim	schlank
ugly	hässlich
good-looking	gut aussehend
old	alt

Key Structures

(jemandem) eine Frage stellen	to ask (somebody) a question
sich eine Frage stellen	to ask oneself a question
Warum stellt sich niemand diese Fragen?	why does nobody ask these questions?
Wenn es doch nur einen einzigen Menschen gäbe, der sich auch diese Fragen stellte, dann würde ich mich nicht so einsam fühlen	I wouldn't feel so lonely if there was just another single person who asked themselves these questions.

FALSCH VERBUNDEN

Understanding the text

alle (pron)	all
also (adv)	well
die Änderung -,-en (nf)	alteration
der Anruf -(e)s,-e (nm)	call
anrufen (v sep*)	to ring, to call
auf etwas warten	to wait for something
auf Wiederhören!	goodbye! (only said on the phone)
die Autowerkstatt -,-¨-en (nf)	garage
beantworten (v)	to answer
die chemische Reinigung (nf)	dry cleaner's
damit (conj)	so that
dann (adv)	then
das (pron)	that
die (pron)	which
die ganze Zeit	all the time
das Ersatzteil -(e)s,-e (nn)	spare part
erwarten (v)	to expect, to be waiting for
etwa (adv)	perhaps
falsch (adj)	wrong
falsch verbunden sein	to have the wrong number
die Fluggesellschaft -,-en (nf)	airline
für (prep)	for
der Gebrauchtwagen -s,- (nm)	second-hand car
guten Tag!	good morning/afternoon!
haben (v*)	to have
hat (v*)	→ haben
he (interj)	hey
hier (adv)	here
ist (v*)	→ sein
jemanden verbinden	to put somebody through
klingeln (v)	to ring
das Kunststopfen -s (nn)	invisible mending
läuten (v)	to ring
die Leute - (npl)	people
mich (pron)	me
mit (prep)	with
müssen (v*)	to have to, must
die Nummer -,-n (nf)	number
der Saum -s,-¨-e (nm)	hem
die Schlosserei -,-en (nf)	locksmith
der Schönheitssalon -s,-s (nm)	beauty salon
sein (v*)	to be
sich verwählen (v)	to misdial, to dial the wrong number
sind (v*)	→ sein
stimmts? 	am I right?
das Telefon -s,-e (nn)	telephone
ununterbrochen (adv)	constantly
verlangen (v)	to ask
wählen (v)	to dial
war (v*)	→sein
wen (pron)	who, whom
wichtig (adj)	important
zu viel	too much

Greetings

to meet somebody	sich mit jemandem treffen
good morning!	guten Morgen!
how are you?	wie geht es Ihnen/dir? wie gehts?
how are things?	wie stehts? 
long time no see	lange nicht gesehen
let me introduce my brother	darf ich Ihnen meinen Bruder vorstellen?/ich möchte dir meinen Bruder vorstellen
she introduced me to her brother	sie hat mich ihrem Bruder vorgestellt
she introduced her brother to me	sie hat mir ihren Bruder vorgestellt
Mary, this is Peter	Mary, das ist Peter
pleased to meet you	(sehr) angenehm (not usually said any more)
parting	der Abschied
to say goodbye to somebody	sich von jemandem verabschieden
goodbye!	auf Wiedersehen!
good night!	gute Nacht!
bye! see you!	tschüss!
see you soon!	bis bald!
see you on Saturday	bis Samstag!
have a good time!	viel Spaß! viel Vergnügen!

Key Structures

Das macht überhaupt nichts, man kann sich auch mal irren.	It doesn't matter at all, we can all make mistakes (sometimes).
Was darf es sein?	Can I help you?
für mich sind die auch nicht	they aren't for me either

die refers to the noun **(Anruf)** in the previous phrase. As there were a number of calls, the speaker is using the plural pronoun **die.**

am Telefon hängen	to be on the phone

This is a colloquial way of saying that someone is spending a long time on the phone (literally: hanging on to the phone).

er hängt schon wieder am Fernseher	he's in front of the telly again.
ich wäre dir sehr dankbar, wenn du die Güte hättest, mich mit … zu verbinden	I'd be most grateful if you'd be good enough to put me through to …

die Güte haben, etwas zu tun is a very polite, rather old-fashioned expression. It can be used sarcastically, as in this case.

DIE PARTY

Understanding the text

abhauen ⓖ (v sep)	to beat it, to leave
anrufen (v sep*)	to ring
aufräumen (v sep)	to tidy up
außer (prep)	except for
der Ausweis -es,-e (nm)	identity card
büffeln (v)	to revise
der Bulle -n,-n ⓖ (nm)	cop
dabei (adv)	during this
dabeihaben (v sep*)	to have on one
denken (v*)	to think
die Eltern (npl)	parents
endlich (adv)	at last, finally
der/die Erste -n,-n (nm/f)	first (one)
erwischen (v)	to catch
festnehmen (v sep*)	to take in, to arrest
Feuer fangen	to catch fire
der Freund -(e)s,-e (nm)	boyfriend
füllen (v)	to fill
ganz (adj)	whole
gegossen (v*)	→ gießen
gekommen (v*)	→ kommen
gerade (adv)	just
gerufen (v*)	→ rufen
geschmissen (v*)	→ schmeißen
gießen (v*)	to pour
gleich (adv)	immediately
die Halogenlampe -,-n (nf)	halogen lamp
hin sein ⓖ	to have had it
immer noch	still
irgendjemand (pron)	somebody
kamen (v*)	→ kommen
der Kochtopf -(e)s,"-e (nm)	saucepan
kommen (v*)	to arrive, to come
man (pron)	one, they
müssen (v*)	to have to
musste, mussten (v*)	→ müssen
natürlich (adv)	of course, naturally
der Notarzt -es,"-e (nm)	(emergency) doctor
ein paar (pron)	a few
die Party -,-s (nf)	party
die Pleite -,-n ⓖ (nf)	flop
die Prüfung -,-en (nf)	exam, examination
rufen (v*)	to call
die Schlägerei -,-en (nf)	fight, punch-up
schließlich (adv)	finally
schmeißen (v*)	to chuck
schnell (adv)	quickly
Selbstmord begehen	to commit suicide
der Teppich -s, -e (nm)	carpet, rug
die Tränengasbombe -,-n (nf)	tear-gas canister
um (conj)	(in order) to
umstoßen (v sep*)	to knock over
der Vielfraß -es,"-e ⓖ (nm)	greedy-guts, greedy pig
völlig (adj)	complete
das Wasser -s (nn)	water
wegfressen ⓖ (v sep*)	to eat up all the food
wegsaufen ⓖ (v sep*)	to drink up all the drink
weil (conj)	because
weinen (v)	to cry
die Wohnung -,-en (nf)	flat
die Zeitschrift -,-en (nf)	magazine

→ Going Out

entertainment	die Unterhaltung
disco	die Disko
nightclub	der Nachtclub
amusement arcade	die Spielhalle
theme park	der Vergnügungspark
festival	das Festival
funfair	der Jahrmarkt
listing, entertainment guide	das Programm
show	die Show
theatre	das Theater
play	das Theaterstück
comedy	die Komödie
opera	die Oper
opera house	die Oper
ballet	das Ballett
concert	das Konzert
classical music	die klassische Musik
film	der Film
documentary film	der Dokumentarfilm
party	die Party, das Fest
to be among friends	unter Freunden sein
let's go to a club	lass uns in einen Club gehen
get-together, meeting-place	der Treff
to have a party	eine Party machen
to go out	ausgehen, weggehen
to go clubbing	in Clubs gehen
to have a celebration	ein Fest feiern
to go to a party	auf ein Fest, eine Party gehen
to have fun	Spaß haben
to meet up with friends in a café	sich mit Freunden im Café treffen

→ Key Structures

The basic meaning of **da** is there, but depending on the context the translation varies.

da sein	to be there or to be here
mein Freund war noch nicht da	my boyfriend wasn't there yet, hadn't arrived yet
war immer noch nicht da	still wasn't there, still hadn't arrived

The basic meaning of **müssen** is must = have to; in the past, this becomes had to in English and in the negative it becomes don't have to

musste gerufen werden	had to be called
seine Eltern mussten angerufen werden	his parents had to be rung, they had to ring his parents
wir mussten aufräumen	we had to tidy up

DAS LEBEN IST LEBENSWERT

Understanding the text

allein (adv)	alone
also gut	well all right then
die Angst -, Ängste (nf)	fear
arbeiten (v)	to work
bist (v*)	→ sein
danke (interj)	thanks
das Leben ist lebenswert	life is worth living
deine Lebensweisheiten	your words of wisdom
du (pron)	you
ein Haufen ⓖ	heaps, lots of
furchtbar (adj)	horrible
haben (v*)	to have
hast (v*)	→ haben
herumreisen (v sep)	to travel around, about
die Hoffnung -,-en (nf)	hope
die Illusion -.-en (nf)	illusion
in (prep)	in
ist (v*)	→ sein
jetzt (adv)	now
die Jugend - (nf)	youth
jung (adj)	young
das Kind -(e)s,-er (nn)	child
leben (v)	to live
das Leben -s,- (nn)	life
leer (adj)	empty
lernen (v)	to learn
die Leute - (npl)	people
die Liebe - (nf)	love
man (pron)	you, one
reist herum (v)	→ herumreisen
sagen (v)	to say
schau mal	look
sein (v*)	to be
sich fühlen (v)	to feel
sich verlieben (v)	to fall in love
sich zu Tode langweilen	to be bored to death
der Spaß -es,¨-e (nm)	fun
ständig (adj)	constant
sterben (v*)	to die
stirbt (v*)	→ sterben
süß (adj)	sweet, cute
das Thema -s,-men (nn)	subject
treffen (v*)	to meet
triffst (v*)	→ treffen
und (conj)	and
viel (pron)	a lot
die Welt -,-en (nf)	world
wenn (conj)	if
zerstören (v)	to destroy
die Zukunft - (nf)	future
der Zustand -(e)s,¨-e (nm)	state

⊡ Education

class	(group of students or pupils) die Klasse; (lesson) die Stunde
a history class	eine Geschichtsstunde
classroom	das Klassenzimmer
pupil	der Schüler/die Schülerin
student	der Student/die Studentin
curriculum	der Lehrplan
exam	die Prüfung
to pass an exam	eine Prüfung bestehen
to fail an exam	durch eine Prüfung fallen
to study law	Jura studieren
nursery school	der Kindergarten, die Vorschule
primary school	die Grundschule
grammar school	das Gymnasium
secondary school	die Hauptschule, die Realschule
comprehensive school	die Gesamtschule
sixth form	die Oberstufe
A-levels	das Abitur
to get good marks	gute Noten bekommen
report	das Zeugnis
to revise for an exam	sich auf eine Prüfung vorbereiten
to go to university	auf die Universität gehen
loan	das Darlehen
adult education	die Erwachsenenbildung
training place	der Ausbildungsplatz, die Lehrstelle

In Germany, **Kindergarten** is for children aged 2 to 6; **Grundschule** (years 1–4) is for pupils aged 6 to 10; **Hauptschule, Realschule** and **Gesamtschule** (years 5–9) are for students aged 11 to 15; **Gymnasium** and **Gesamtschule** (years 10–13) are for students aged 16 to 19. **Mittlere Reife** (similar to GCSE) is taken after ten years of schooling. You take **Abitur**, which is similar to A-levels, at a **Gymnasium** or a **Gesamtschule.**
The compulsory mimimum period of education in Germany is nine years. Students who leave school with the **Hauptschulabschluss** (secondary-school leaving certificate) usually go on to do an apprenticeship.

⊡ Key Structures

Was ist los?	What's the matter?
Geht es um … ?	Is it about … ?
worum geht es hier?	what is this all about?
es geht um unsere Ferien	it's about our holiday
in this construction the verb **gehen** means to concern, to be about	
in der Welt herumreisen	to travel all over the world
ein Klotz am Bein	(literally: a block of wood tied to your leg) a millstone round your neck
es gibt kein Zurück mehr	there's no going back
jetzt fühle ich mich erst richtig gut	now I feel really great

YELLOW SUBMARINE

Understanding the text

bist (v*)	→ sein
dass (conj)	that
dir (pron)	you
du (pron)	you
eine fangen	to get a clip round the ear
haben (v*)	to have
hast (v*)	→ haben
ich (pron)	I
ich auch nicht	nor me
ihn (pron)	it
in Englisch	for English
ja (adv)	yes
jetzt (adv)	now
die Kassette -,-n (nf)	cassette
kennen (v*)	to know
kennst (v*)	→ kennen
die Klassenarbeit -,-en (nf)	(class) test
das Lied -(e)s,-er (nn)	song
los (adv)	come on
man (pron)	one
morgen früh	tomorrow morning
neben (prep)	next to
ruhig (adj)	quiet
sein (v*)	to be

sitz/sitzt (v*)	→ sitzen
sitzen (v*)	to sit
so (adv)	so
stinken (v*)	to smell
stinkst (v*)	→ stinken
der Text -(e)s,-e (nm)	lyrics, words
über (prep)	about
und (conj)	and
vergessen (v*)	to forget
völlig (adv)	completely, totally
von (prep)	of
wann (adv)	when
was (pron)	what
wenn (conj)	if

 Family

father	der Vater
mother	die Mutter
grandfather	der Großvater
grandmother	die Großmutter
brother	der Bruder
sister	die Schwester
son	der Sohn
daughter	die Tochter
uncle	der Onkel
aunt	die Tante
nephew	der Neffe
niece	die Nichte
parents	die Eltern (n pl)
father-in-law	der Schwiegervater
mother-in-law	die Schwiegermutter
brother-in-law	der Schwager
sister-in-law	die Schwägerin
son-in-law	der Schwiegersohn
daughter-in-law	die Schwiegertochter
stepfather	der Stiefvater
stepmother	die Stiefmutter
stepbrother	der Stiefbruder
stepsister	die Stiefschwester
cousin	der Vetter/die Kusine
twins	die Zwillinge (nm pl)
relation	der/die Verwandte
baby	das Baby
our relations	unsere Verwandten (pl), unsere Verwandschaft (sing)
childminder	die Tagesmutter
to get married	heiraten
to marry somebody	jemanden heiraten
married	verheiratet
to live together	zusammenleben
to divorce	sich scheiden lassen
divorced	geschieden
to bring up a child	ein Kind erziehen

Key Structures

The imperative is used to give orders. All imperatives should be followed by an exclamation mark.

Halt die Klappe!	Shut up!
Los, sing!	Come on, sing!

The du form of the imperative ends in -e (halte), but the -e is usually dropped, especially in colloquial speech.

lauf!	run!
komm sofort!	come at once!

du singst so falsch, dass es einem schlecht wird (literally, you are singing so wrongly, it makes one ill) you're such a terrible singer, it makes me sick

the pronoun **einen** can be translated with you or one

das macht einen müde — it makes you tired

DIE KRISE

Understanding the text

also (adv)	well
also gut	all right then
das Appartement –s,–s (nn)	flat, apartment
ätzend ◎ (adj)	disgusting, awful
dabei (adv)	and yet
dass (conj)	that
du (pron)	you
ein/eine/ein (art)	a, an
einfach (adv)	simply
erzählen (v)	to tell
fallen (v*)	to go down
finden (v*)	to find
für (prep)	for
gefunden (v*)	→ finden
gekauft (v)	→ kaufen
der Geschirrspüler –s,– (nm)	dishwasher
gesehen (v*)	→ sehen
für die Hälfte	for half the price, (at) half price
ihre (pron)	her
in der Nähe	near
das Jahr –(e)s,–e (nn)	year
kaufen (v)	to buy
sich knutschen ◎ (v)	to kiss, to smooch
sich mit jemandem knutschen	to smooch with somebody
kriegen (v)	to get
kriegt (v)	→ kriegen
die Krise –,–n (nf)	crisis
letzter/letzte/letztes (adj)	last

die Mark – (nf)	mark
die Marke –,–n (nf)	make
mein (adj)	my
meinen (v)	to think
mit (prep)	with
der Onkel –s,– (nm)	uncle
der Preis –es,–e (nm)	price
pro (prep)	per
der Quadratmeter –s,– (nm)	square metre
raten (v*)	to guess
sagen (v)	to say
die Schule –,–n (nf)	school
sehen (v*)	to see
mit jemandem Schluss machen ◎	to split up/finish with somebody
das Spatzengehirn –s,–e (nn)	birdbrain
so was = so etwas	something like that
ständig (adv)	all the time
ungefähr (adv)	about, approximately
unglaublich (adj)	incredible, unbelievable
was (pron)	what
welcher/welche/welches (adj)	which
wie (adv)	how
wie viel	how many, how much
die Wohnung –,–en (nf)	flat
zahlen (v)	to pay
zusammen (adv)	together
zusammenziehen (v sep*)	to move in together

⊡ Key Structures

wie viel	how much or how many
wie viel hat das gekostet?	how much was it, how much did it cost?
wie viel (or wie viele) Zimmer?	how many rooms?

but:

um wie viel Uhr kommt sie?	(at) what time is she coming?
zusammenziehen (v sep*)	to move in together

when the verb **zusammenziehen** means moving in together, it is formed with **sein**

sie sind zusammen gezogen	they moved in together

but:

when **zusammenziehen** means to pull or draw together, it takes **haben**

sie hat das Netz zusammengezogen	she pulled the net tight

⊡ Home

flat, apartment	**die Wohnung**
studio flat	**das Studio**
to share a house/flat	**in einer Wohngemeinschaft leben**
co-owner	**der Miteigentümer/die Miteigentümerin**
tenant	**der Mieter/die Mieterin**
to rent a house/flat	**ein Haus/eine Wohnung mieten**
to let a house/flat	**ein Haus/eine Wohnung vermieten**
to live in the country	**auf dem Land wohnen**
city centre	**das Stadtzentrum**
suburb	**der Vorort**
in the suburbs of Berlin	**in den Berliner Vororten**
block of flats	**der Wohnblock**
double room	**das Doppelzimmer**
single room	**das Einzelzimmer**
a room with a sea view	**ein Zimmer mit Aussicht aufs Meer**
fitted kitchen	**die Einbauküche**
sitting room	**das Wohnzimmer**
bedroom	**das Schlafzimmer**
bathroom	**das Badezimmer**
dining room	**das Esszimmer**
toilet	**die Toilette**
loo	**das Klo**
rent	**die Miete**
garden	**der Garten**
garage	**die Garage**
to pay a deposit	**eine Kaution zahlen**

FREIZEIT

20

Understanding the text

alle (pron)		all
auch (adv)		also, too
bleiben (v*)		to stay
bloß nicht		no way, under no circumstances
da (adv)		here, there
das (pron)		that
das ist		it's
das Fernsehen –s (nn)		television
die Freizeit – (nf)		leisure
gehen (v*)		to go
das Geld –(e)s,–er (nn)		money
haben (v*)		to have
hallo (interj)		hello
hassen (v)		to hate
heiß (adj)		hot
hören (v)		to listen to
ihr (pron)		you
ins = in das		to the
irgendein (pron)		any
ist (v*)		→ sein
kann (v*)		→ können
kaputt (adj)		broken
das Kaufhaus –es,–¨er (nn)		department store
kein (adj)		no
das Kino –s,–s (nn)		cinema
können (v*)		to be able to
lahm ⓔ (adj)		boring, dull
laufen (v*)		to be on, to be showing
läuft (v*)		→ laufen
machen (v)		to do
der Mist –(e)s (nm)		rubbish
mit dir		with you
die Musik – (nf)		music
die Mutter –,–¨ (nf)		mother
ne ⓔ (adv)		no
neu (adj)		new
nur (adv)		only
ob (conj)		whether, if
oder (conj)		or
der Plattenladen –s,–¨ (nm)		music shop
sein (v*)		to be
sich langweilen (v)		to be bored
spielen (v)		to play
das Tennis – (nn)		tennis
das Video –s,–s (nn)		video (cassette)
der Videorekorder –s,– (nm)		video recorder
vielleicht (adv)		perhaps
was (pron)		what
weit (adv)		far
wir (pron)		we
wir könnten		we could
zu (adv)		too
zur Zeit		at the moment

Pastimes

to play tennis/squash/badminton	Tennis/Squash/Federball spielen
I love swimming/playing baseball	ich schwimme gern/spiele gern Baseball
where can we play golf/go riding/play football?	wo kann man Golf spielen/reiten/ Fußball spielen?
I want to do aerobics	ich will Aerobic machen
is there a football match on today?	gibt es heute ein Fußballspiel?
to play computer games	Computerspiele spielen
to watch TV	fernsehen
we watched TV all evening	wir sahen den ganzen Abend fern
the game is on television	das Spiel kommt im Fernsehen
what's on at the cinema?	was läuft im Kino?
to surf the Net	im Internet surfen
to listen to music	Musik hören
CD	die CD
record	die Platte
tape	die Kassette
to tape something	etwas auf Kassette aufnehmen
album	das Album
the new X-album has just come out	das neue X-Album ist gerade erschienen
I like reading/listening to music	ich lese gern/höre gern Musik
I like yoga	ich mache gern Yoga
I love a game of Tennis	ich spiele sehr gern Tennis, Tennis macht mir richtig Spaß
I don't like swimming	ich gehe nicht gern schwimmen
I like painting/programming/ computer games	ich male gern/programmiere gern/ spiele gern Computerspiele
I hate chess	ich hasse Schach, ich kann Schach nicht ausstehen
there's nothing I hate more than doing homework	nichts hasse ich mehr als Hausaufgaben machen

Key Structures

was machen wir?	what are we going to do?
vielleicht gibts was im Fernsehen	perhaps there's something on television
es läuft nur Mist	there's only rubbish on

The general translation for the verb **laufen** is to run, but in the context of films, programmes, shows or plays it means to be on or showing. The verb **geben** is used similarly in the context of films and programmes.

gibts was im Fernsehen?	is there anything on television?
was gibts im Fernsehen?	what's on television?
gibts das schon auf Video?	is it out on video yet?
ich bleib lieber hier	I'd prefer to stay here or I'd rather stay here.

lieber is used when saying what you prefer.

ich auch	me too
ich seh mal nach, ob sie da ist	I'll (go and) see if she's there
ich verbinde Sie (used on the phone)	I'll put you through
ich habe wahnsinnig viel zu tun	I'm terribly busy

KOMMUNIKATION

Understanding the text

arbeiten (v)	to work
auch (adv)	also, too
auf (prep)	on
aufkleben (v sep)	to stick on
beide (adj)	both
besetzt (adj)	engaged
bis jetzt	up to now, so far
der Briefumschlag –(e)s,̈-e (nm)	envelope
dass (conj)	that
durchkommen (v sep*)	to get through
einfach (adj)	easy, simple
einwerfen (v sep*)	to post, to mail
das Fax –,-(e) (nn)	fax
die Faxnummer –,-n (nf)	fax number
die Frau –,-en (nf)	wife
das Handy –s,-s (nn)	mobile (phone)
die Haustür –,-en (nf)	front door
heutzutage (adv)	nowadays
hingehen (v sep*)	to go (there)
ist (v*)	→ sein
ist besetzt	is engaged
kennen (v*)	to know
die Kommunikation – (nf)	communication
machen (v)	to do
mit jemandem sprechen	to speak/talk to somebody
na (interj)	well
natürlich (adv)	of course
nichts (pron)	nothing
schreiben (v*)	to write
sein (adj)	his
sein (v*)	to be
seit drei Stunden	for three hours
sind (v*)	→ sein
so (adv)	so
sollen (v*)	should
sprechen (v*)	to speak, to talk
ständig (adv)	constantly
stecken (v)	to put
der Stiefbruder –s,̈- (nm)	stepbrother
der Stiefvater –s,̈- (nm)	stepfather
die Stunde –,-n (nf)	hour
die Telefonnummer –,-n (nf)	phone number
versuchen (v)	to try
von (prep)	of
was (pron)	what
weißt (v*)	→ wissen
wenn (conj)	when
wissen (v*)	to know
die Zahlenkombination –,-en (nf)	(number) code
zu (prep)	to
zu Hause	at home
zu jemandem hingehen	to go to somebody

⬌ Communication

telephone	das Telefon
fax machine	das Faxgerät, das Telefax
fax number	die Faxnummer
fax message	das Fax, das Telefax
to receive/send a fax	ein Fax empfangen/senden
e-mail	die E-Mail
telecommunications	die Telekommunikation, das Fernmeldewesen
phone card	die Telefonkarte
phone box	die Telefonzelle
mobile (phone)	das Handy, das Mobiltelefon
pager	der Piepser
intercom	die Gegensprechanlage
message	die Nachricht
web site	die Web-Site
computer print-out	der Computerausdruck
post office	die Post
postman	der Briefträger
courier	der Bote
letter	der Brief
parcel	das Paket
post-restante	postlagernd
to send a letter poste-restante	jdm postlagernd schreiben
PO box	das Postfach
to have one's mail forwarded	sich die Post nachschicken lassen
to send something by post/mail	etwas mit der/per Post schicken
the press	die Presse
radio	das Radio
media	die Medien (pl)
television	das Fernsehen
news	die Nachrichten (pl)
daily paper	die Tageszeitung
magazine	die Zeitschrift
to be easy to reach	leicht erreichbar sein
she can be reached/contacted by phone	sie ist telefonisch erreichbar
to notify/inform somebody	jemanden verständigen
to communicate	sich verständigen

⬌ Key Structures

Das liegt daran, dass …	It's because …
Das kannst du der Frau seines Stiefbruders zuschreiben	you can blame his stepbrother's wife for it
jemandem die Schuld zuschreiben	to blame somebody
wenn ich mich mit jemandem in Verbindung setzen will	when I want to get in touch with somebody
Das sollte ihn schon nachdenklich stimmen	that should really make him think
Auf die Post ist auch kein Verlass	you can't rely on the post either

IN MODE

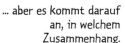

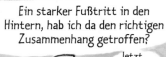

Understanding the text

aber (conj)	but
ach (int)	oh
also (adv)	well, all right then
auch (adv)	also, too
aus der Mode (sein)	(to be) out
die Birne –,-n (nf)	bulb
bitte (adv)	please
die blaue	the blue one
die CD –,-s (nf)	CD
du (pron)	you
ein/eine/ein (art)	a, an
es kommt darauf an	it depends (on)
famos (adj)	splendid
die Fete –,-n ⓢ (nf)	party
finden (v*)	to find
der Fußtritt –(e)s,-e (nm)	kick
getroffen (v*)	→ **treffen**
gut (adj)	all right, OK
der Hintern –s,- ⓢ (nm)	behind, bottom
in Mode (sein)	(to be) in
jetzt (adv)	now
der Kaffee –s,-s (nm)	coffee
die Lösung –,-en (nf)	solution
die Mami –,-s (nf)	mummy
der Mann –(e)s,¨-er (nm)	man
die Mutti –,-s (nf)	mum
sich (dat) **Mühe geben**	to try hard
nicht (adv)	not
prima (adj)	great
richtig (adj)	right, correct
sagen (v)	to say
schon wieder	again
sich gekränkt fühlen	to feel hurt
sogar (adv)	even
stark (adj)	fantastic, brilliant
treffen (v*)	to hit (on)
tu mir einen Gefallen	do me a favour
überhaupt nicht	not at all
verstehen (v*)	to understand
was (pron)	what
weiß (v*)	→ **wissen**
welcher/welche/welches (pron)	which (one)
wissen (v*)	to know
der Zusammenhang –s,¨-e (nm)	context

⮊ Key Structures

seit Ewigkeiten	for ages
"prima" sagt man schon seit Ewigkeiten nicht mehr	"great" has been out for ages
ich habe ihn seit Ewigkeiten nicht mehr gesehen	I haven't seen him for ages
man kann sagen, was man will	you can say anything, whatever you like.

In this case **was** means whatever or anything.

Jetzt fühlst du dich gekränkt, oder?	Now you're feeling hurt, aren't you?

Oder is used in questions at the end of a sentence and indicates an element of doubt.

das ist doch erlaubt, oder?	that is allowed, isn't it?
das hört sich gut an, oder?	that sounds good, don't you think?
er kommt doch mit, oder?	he's coming, isn't he?

⮊ Approval and Disapproval

all right	ist gut, okay
great!	klasse! prima! toll!
you are right	Sie haben Recht
to give one's approval to something	seine Zustimmung zu etwas geben
to agree with somebody (about something)	mit jemandem (über etwas) übereinstimmen
I agree with you	ich stimme Ihnen zu
we agree with your decision	wir sind mit Ihrer Entscheidung einverstanden
I agree with you on that	da bin ich ganz deiner/Ihrer Meinung
I couldn't agree more	ich bin ganz deiner/Ihrer Meinung
that's a great idea	das ist wirklich eine gute Idee
not bad at all	nicht schlecht
well done!	gut gemacht!
I liked the way you …	ich finde es gut, dass du…
I don't agree that …	ich bin damit nicht einverstanden , dass …
I disagree with him	ich stimme nicht mit ihm überein
on the contrary	im Gegenteil
Peter has agreed to pay	Peter sagt, dass er zahlt
to refuse to do something	sich weigern, etwas zu tun
to refuse somebody permission	jemandem die Erlaubnis verweigern
he refused to pay	er weigerte sich zu zahlen
no way!	auf keinen Fall!
it's a real shame that …	es ist wirklich schade, dass …

DER BESUCH

Ach, du bist es, mein Schatz. Na, das ist aber ein seltener Besuch!

Deine Mutter habe ich zuletzt am 28. Oktober bei der Beerdigung deines Großonkels gesehen.

Deinen Vater habe ich zuletzt am 9. November gesehen. Da hat er mich zu meinem Geburtstag zum Essen eingeladen ...

... obwohl ich ja eigentlich lieber ins Kino gegangen wäre. Na ja, vergeben und vergessen. Aber wie gehts dir?

Ich...

Deinen Bruder Martin habe ich zuletzt ... ach nein, dein Bruder heißt ja Max. Ich verwechsele ihn doch immer mit Peters Sohn.

Also den Max habe ich am 1. November gesehen. Und Martin, ja den habe ich am 4. November um 15 Uhr gesehen ...

... da bin ich mit ihm im Park gewesen. Um 16.30 habe ich ihn dann zurückgebracht und seitdem nichts!

Wie Katja – sie ist am 7. um 17 Uhr zu Besuch gekommen und um 18.30 war sie schon wieder weg.

Susi ist immer darauf aus, mich zu besuchen. Aber sie war zuletzt am 25. Oktober da, und da hat sie mich mit ihrem Gequassel furchtbar gelangweilt!

Was wollte ich noch sagen? Ja, und du, du hast dich auch seit dem 8. November um 18 Uhr nicht mehr blicken lassen ... nur einmal kurz angerufen.

Und außerdem kommst du mich ja nie besuchen.

Understanding the text

anrufen (v sep*)	to phone
außerdem (adv)	besides
die **Beerdigung** –,–en (nf)	funeral
der **Besuch** –(e)s, –e (nm)	visit
der **Bruder** –s,̈– (nm)	brother
da (adv)	here, there
darauf aus sein	to be keen on
eigentlich (adv)	actually
einladen (v sep*)	to invite
einmal (adv)	once
das **Essen** –s,– (nn)	meal
furchtbar (adv)	terribly
der **Geburtstag** –(e)s,–e (nm)	birthday
gegangen (v*)	→ gehen
gehen (v*)	to go
das **Gequassel** –s (nn)	jabbering
der **Großonkel** –s,– (nm)	great uncle
heißen (v*)	to be called
immer (adv)	always
das **Kino** –s,–s (nn)	cinema
kommen (v*)	to come
langweilen (v)	to bore
mit (prep)	with
die **Mutter** –,̈– (nf)	mother
nichts (pron)	nothing
nie (adv)	never
November –s,– (nm)	November
obwohl (conj)	although
Oktober –s,– (nm)	October
der **Park** –s,–s (nm)	park
sagen (v)	to say
der **Schatz** –es,̈–e (nm)	darling
schon (adv)	already
sehen (v*)	to see
sein (v*)	to be
seit (conj)	since
seitdem (adv)	since
selten (adj)	rare
sich blicken lassen	to put in an appearance
der **Sohn** –s,̈–e (nm)	son
der **Vater** –s,̈– (nm)	father
verwechseln (v)	to mix up
weg (adv)	gone
weg sein	to be gone
wie (conj)	like, as
wie gehts dir?	how are you?
wieder (adv)	again
wollen (v*)	to want
zuletzt (adv)	last
zurückbringen (v sep*)	to bring back

⮕ Dates

on Monday	**am Montag**
on Monday evening	**am Montagabend**
on Tuesday(s)	**dienstags**
on Tuesday evenings	**dienstagabends**
we usually play tennis on Wednesday evening(s)	**mittwochabends spielen wir meistens Tennis**
every Monday evening	**jeden Montagabend**
next Tuesday evening/morning	**nächsten Dienstagabend/Dienstagmorgen**
this/yesterday/tomorrow evening	**heute/gestern/morgen Abend**
this morning	**heute früh**
next Friday	**nächsten Freitag**
Saturday morning	**Samstagmorgen** or **Samstag früh**
on Saturday mornings	**samstagmorgens**
in January	**im Januar**
next February	**nächsten Februar**
last March	**letzten März**
in early April	**Anfang April**
in late May	**Ende Mai**
in 1999	**1999**
in 2000	**im Jahr 2000**
from 2000	**ab dem Jahr 2000**
since the 1st of May	**seit dem 1. Mai**
she came to see me on the 22nd of June	**sie hat mich am 22. Juni besucht**
the last time I saw her was the 13th of November	**ich habe sie zuletzt am 13. November gesehen**
what is the date today?	**der Wievielte ist heute?**
what is the day today?	**welcher Tag ist heute?**
it's the first of December	**heute ist der erste Dezember**

⮕ Days of the week and months

Monday	**Montag** (nm)
Tuesday	**Dienstag** (nm)
Wednesday	**Mittwoch** (nm)
Thursday	**Donnerstag** (nm)
Friday	**Freitag** (nm)
Saturday	**Samstag** or **Sonnabend** (nm)
Sunday	**Sonntag** (nm)
January	**Januar** (nm)
February	**Februar** (nm)
March	**März** (nm)
April	**April** (nm)
May	**Mai** (nm)
June	**Juni** (nm)
July	**Juli** (nm)
August	**August** (nm)
September	**September** (nm)
October	**Oktober** (nm)
November	**November** (nm)
December	**Dezember** (nm)

⮕ Key Structures

the adverb **da** (indicating time and meaning then, at that moment) is often used in colloquial speech but is usually not translated.

    da hat er mich zum Essen eingeladen   he invited me for a meal

Depending on the context, the adverb **da** (indicating location) can mean here or there.

    sie war zuletzt am 25. Oktober da   the last time she was here was on 25/10.

    da bin ich   here I am

ich wäre lieber ins Kino gegangen   I would have preferred to go to the cinema

lieber is the comparative of the adverb **gern: gern, lieber, am liebsten** (superlative)

    etwas gern tun   to like doing something

    etwas lieber tun   to prefer doing something

    etwas am liebsten tun   to like doing something best

vergeben und vergessen!   let's hear no more about it!

DER AMERIKANISCHE TRAUM

Understanding the text

der **Abstecher** –s,– (nm)	side-trip
acht (adj)	eight
alt (adj)	old
amerikanisch (adj)	American
aussehen (v sep*)	to look like
außerdem (adv)	in addition, as well as
aussieht (v*)	→ aussehen
clever (adj)	clever
cool (adj)	brilliant
der **Daddy** –s,–s (nm)	daddy, father
die **Dame** –,–n (nf)	lady
drei (adj)	three
einladen (v sep*)	to invite
endlich (adv)	at last
entwachsen (v*)	to outgrow, to grow out of
das **Highlight** –(s),–s (nn)	highlight
hörst zu (v)	→ zuhören
das **Jahr** –(e)s,–e (nn)	year
die **Jazzmusik** – (nf)	jazz, jazz music
jeder/jede/jedes (adj)	every
jetzt (adv)	now
der **Juli** –(s),–s (nm)	July
jung (adj)	young
der **Junge** –n,–n	lad, boy
kennen lernen (v)	to get to know
klasse (adj)	great
der **Kumpel** –s,– (nm)	mate, pal
der **Kurzbesuch** –(e)s,–e (nm)	short visit

ladet ein (v*)	→ einladen
der **Megastore** –s,–s (nm)	megastore
mitkommen (v sep*)	to come (along) too
das **Museum** –s,–seen (nn)	museum
muss (v*)	→ müssen
müssen (v*)	to have (got) to
okay (interj)	OK
der **Plan** –s,ˮ–e (nm)	plan
die **Ranch** –,–(e)s (nf)	ranch
reden (v)	to talk
die **Reise** –,–n (nf)	journey
richtig (adv)	properly
ruf zurück (v*)	→ zurückrufen
die **Rundreise** –,–n (nf)	tour
das **Shopping** –s (nn)	shopping
später (adv)	later
die **Staaten** (npl)	the States
das **Studio** –s,–s (nn)	studio
der **Tag** –(e)s,–e (nm)	day
der **Traum** –s,ˮ–e (nm)	dream
überhaupt (adv)	at all
unser (adj)	our
weil (conj)	because
die **Woche** –,–n (nf)	week
zuhören (v sep)	to listen
zurückrufen (v sep*)	to call back

⬄ Key Structures

da bin ich	here I am, here we are
ich kann jetzt nicht mir dir telefonieren	I can't talk to you (on the phone) now
bis gleich	speak to you later, see you later

The verb **zuhören** is a separable verb and takes the dative.

ich muss jetzt meinem Vater zuhören	I've got to listen to my father now
hörst du mir überhaupt zu?	are you listening to me?
muss ich mitkommen?	do I have to come too?
seit + dative	since or for

For an action starting in the past and going on to the present, the present tense is used after **seit**.

Er ladet mich seit zehn Jahren jedes Jahr ein — he's been inviting me every year for the last ten years

With a negative or a series of actions the perfect is used, as in English.
Er hat ihn seit zehn Jahren nicht mehr gesehen — he hasn't seen him for ten years

der hat einen 17-jährigen Sohn — he has a 17-year-old son
17-jährig = siebzehnjährig
eine dreiwöchige Reise = eine 3-wöchige Reise — a three-week trip

Was sagst du dazu? — what do you think?

⬄ Travelling

airport	**der Flughafen**
(railway) station	**der Bahnhof**
coach station	**der Busbahnhof**
port	**der Hafen**
hotel	**das Hotel**
pub	**die Kneipe**
youth hostel	**die Jugendherberge**
guest house	**die Pension**
vacancies!	**Zimmer zu vermieten! Zimmer frei!**
no vacancies!	**belegt!**
half board	**die Halbpension**
a single room	**ein Einzelzimmer**
a double room	**ein Doppelzimmer**
a room with three beds	**ein Dreibettzimmer**
an en-suite room	**ein Zimmer mit Bad**
reception desk	**die Rezeption**
to ask for a room at reception	**an der Rezeption nach einem Zimmer fragen**
full board	**die Vollpension**
breakfast	**das Frühstück**
do you have a double room?	**haben Sie ein Doppelzimmer?**
we are full	**wir sind belegt**
does that include breakfast?	**ist das mit Frühstück?**
to book a room for 3 nights	**ein Zimmer für 3 Nächte reservieren lassen**
can you book a room for me?	**können Sie für mich ein Zimmer reservieren?**
how much is the room?	**was kostet das Zimmer?**

KNAUSERIG

Understanding the text

abmachen (v sep)	to take off	
anfangen (v sep*)	to do	
ätzend ◎ (adj)	disgusting, awful	
danke (schön) (adv)	thanks, thank you	
denken (v*)	to think	
für (prep)	for	
furchtbar (adv)	terribly	
geil (interj)	cool, brilliant	
das **Geschenk –(e)s,–e** (nn)	present	
geschenkt (v)	→ schenken	
haben (v*)	to have	
hat (v*)	→ haben	
ist (v*)	→ sein	
kann (v*)	→ können	
das **Kind –es,–er** (nn)	child	
klein (adj)	little, small	
die **Kleinigkeit –,–en** (nf)	small gift, present	
knauserig (adj)	stingy	
können (v*)	to be able, can	
die **Leute** (npl)	people	
der **Liebling –s,–e** (nm)	darling	
machen (v)	to do	
man (pron)	you, one	
Mark – (nf)	mark	
muss (v*)	→ müssen	
müssen (v*)	to have to	
natürlich (adv)	of course	
nett (adj)	nice	
der **Preis –es,–e** (nm)	price	
sagen (v)	to say	
schenken (v)	to give (as a present)	
schon (adv)	already	
sein (v*)	to be	
sich freuen (v)	to be pleased	
sich lohnen (v)	to be worth it	
sind (v*)	→ sein	
der **Sohn –(e)s,¨–e** (nm)	son	
sowieso (adv)	anyway	
die **Tante –,–n** (nf)	aunt	
umtauschen (v sep)	to change	
der **Vati –s,–s** (nm)	dad	
wahnsinnig (adv)	terribly	
war (v*)	→ sein	
was (pron)	what	
wenn (conj)	if	
werden (v*)	will	
wie (conj)	like, as	
wird (v*)	→ werden	
wirklich (adv)	really	
zu viel	too much	

⇥ Money

Will earns 2,500 marks a month	Will verdient monatlich 2 500 DM (DM = Deutsche Mark)
a well-paid job	eine gut bezahlte Stellung
I've been given a pay rise	ich habe eine Gehaltserhöhung bekommen
bank	die Bank
bank account	das Bankkonto
bank balance	der Kontostand
savings	Ersparnisse (n pl)
savings bank	die Sparkasse
building society	die Bausparkasse
to make a deposit	Geld einzahlen
to make a withdrawal	Geld abheben
cashpoint, cash machine	der Geldautomat
I'll get some money from the cash machine	ich hole mir Geld vom Automaten
to change money	Geld wechseln
he wants to change 100 pounds into marks	er möchte 100 Pfund in Mark wechseln
a £100 cheque	ein Scheck über 100 Pfund
I want to cash this cheque	ich möchte diesen Scheck einlösen
Eurocheque	der Euroscheck
PIN (number)	die Geheimnummer
small change	das Wechselgeld
coin	die Münze
cash	das Bargeld
banknote	der Geldschein
cheque book	das Scheckbuch
credit card	die Kreditkarte
cheque card, cash card	die Scheckkarte
to insert a coin	eine Münze einwerfen
insert your card	Karte einführen

⇥ Key Structures

es lohnt sich wirklich nicht, ihm was zu schenken	it's really not worth giving him presents
was = etwas	
das darf nicht wahr sein!	I don't believe it!
Beachte sie nicht!	Ignore her!
Jetzt reichts aber ◎	That's enough

reichts = reicht es
This contraction is used in colloquial German. Before the recent spelling reform the dropped letter e was replaced by an apostrophe (reicht's).

VERLIEBT

Understanding the text

alle (pron pl)	everybody
auf jemanden stehen	to be really keen on somebody
ausquatschen (v)	to let out
bescheuert (adj)	stupid
bestimmt (adv)	certainly
bist (v*)	→ **sein**
cool (adj)	great, cool
dann (adv)	then
das ist egal	that doesn't make any difference
das stimmt nicht	it's not true
dass (conj)	that
du spinnst	you're nuts
ehrlich (adv)	honestly
ein bisschen	a little, a bit
die Entscheidung –,-en (nf)	decision
erstens (adv)	firstly
das Feingefühl –(e)s (nn)	sensitivity
die Frage –,-n (nf)	question
furchtbar (adv)	terribly
geküsst (v)	→ **küssen**
groß (adj)	big
haben (v*)	to have
die Hälfte –,-n (nf)	half
hat (v*)	→ **haben**
immer (adv)	always
die Inliner (nm pl)	rollerblades, inline skates
ist (v*)	→ **sein**
jemanden nerven (v)	to get on somebody's nerves
jung (adj)	young
kann (v*)	→ **können**
kaufen (v)	to buy
können (v*)	can (to be able)
küssen (v)	to kiss
machen (v)	to do
machst (v)	→ **machen**
mal = einmal (adv)	once
miteinander (adv)	with each other, together
nur (adv)	only
sagen (v)	to say
schon (adv)	yet
sein (v*)	to be
selbst (adv)	even
sich amüsieren (v)	to have fun
der Softie –s,-s (nm)	wimp
sonst noch Fragen?	any other questions?
stinklangweilig (adj)	deadly boring
der Takt –(e)s (nm)	tact, tactfulness
der Typ –en or –s,-en (nm)	bloke, guy
verknallt sein ©	to be in love
verstehen (v*)	to understand
wann (adv)	when
weggehen (v sep*)	to go out
weil (conj)	because
wenn (conj)	when
wenn du nichts dagegen hast	if you don't mind
wissen (v*)	to know
zugegeben	admittedly
zusammen (adv)	together
zwar (adv)	admittedly
zweitens (adv)	secondly

⇨ Love and Relationships

friendship	**die Freundschaft**
to make friends with somebody	**mit jemandem Freundschaft schließen**
friend	**der Freund/die Freundin**
boyfriend/girlfriend	**der Freund/die Freundin**
he's got a new girlfriend	**er hat eine neue Freundin, ein neues Mädchen**
acquaintance	**der/die Bekannte**
who's she going out with now?	**mit wem geht sie jetzt?**
to chat somebody up	**jemanden anmachen** ©
to fancy somebody	**auf jemanden abfahren** ©
where shall we meet?	**wo treffen wir uns?**
hi	**Hallo**
what's your telephone number?	**wie ist deine Telefonnummer?**
do you fancy going to the cinema/ for a meal?	**hast du Lust ins Kino zu gehen/ essen zu gehen?**
to get off with a girl	**ein Mädchen abschleppen** ©
to be in love (with somebody)	**(in jemanden) verliebt sein**
to kiss	**sich küssen**
to shake hands with somebody	**jemandem die Hand geben**
we shook hands	**wir haben uns die Hand gegeben**
to be fond of somebody	**jemanden sehr gern mögen**
I like him	**ich mag ihn**
to get on well	**gut miteinander auskommen, sich gut verstehen**
to hate somebody	**jemanden nicht ausstehen können**
he misses her	**sie fehlt ihm**

⇨ Key Structures

...was du an diesem bescheuerten Nick findest	...what you see in this stupid Nick
du bist eben auf 'ner andren Wellenlänge	we're just not on the same wavelength
auf 'ner = auf einer	on a
ich steh auf so Typen	I'm really keen on those (sort of) guys
Über so was zu reden ist mir peinlich	it's embarrassing to talk about things like that
wann wird die große Entscheidung getroffen?	when are you making the big decision?

the impersonal construction adds a touch of irony to the question.

sind ja nicht gerade deine Stärke	aren't exactly your strong point

ja is just a filler word and is not normally translated

HALLO?

Understanding the text

der **Afrikaner** –s,– (nm)	African
angehen (v sep*)	to tackle
anrufen (v sep*)	to call
die **Anweisung** –,–en (nf)	instruction
ausmachen (v sep)	to arrange
das **Auto** –s,–s (nn)	car
Deutschland –s (nn)	Germany
eben (adv)	just
einen Treffpunkt ausmachen	to arrange a meeting-place
einmal (adv)	once
erster/erste/erstes (adj)	first
genau (adj)	precise, exact
gerade (adv)	just
geschält (adj)	peeled
die **Großmutter** –,˝– (nf)	grandmother
gut!	right!
hallo (int)	hello
das **Handy** –s,–s (nn)	mobile phone
heute (adv)	today
ins Krankenhaus eingeliefert werden	to be taken to hospital
ins Wasser tun	to put into water
jdm etw sagen	to tell somebody something
jdn ausfindig machen	to find somebody
jetzt (adv)	now
jetzt hör mal zu!	now listen!
die **Kartoffel** –,–n (nf)	potato
klein (adj)	little
kochen (v)	to boil
krank (adj)	ill, sick
das **Krankenhaus** –es,˝–er (nn)	hospital
lassen (v*)	to let
liegen (v*)	to lie
das **Medikament** –(e)s,–e (nn)	medicine
mit (prep)	with
die **Mutter** –,˝– (nf)	mother
neben (prep)	next to
noch (ein)mal	again
die **Prise** –,–n (nf)	pinch
sagen (v)	to say
das **Salz** –es,–e (nn)	salt
schälen (v)	to peel
schicken (v)	to send
schon einmal	before
die **Schwester** –,–n (nf)	sister
sehen (v*)	to see
sponsern (v)	to sponsor
stehlen (v*)	to steal
stören (v)	to disturb
der **Topf** –(e)s,˝–e (nm)	saucepan
der **Treffpunkt** –s,–e (nm)	meeting-place
der **Unterricht** –s,–e (nm)	lessons
der **Vater** –s,˝– (nm)	father
die **Viertelstunde** –,–n (nf)	quarter of an hour
das **Wasser** –s,– (nn)	water
wiederholen (v)	to repeat
wo (adv)	where
wollen (v*)	to want
die **Zahlungsbilanz** –,–en (nf)	balance of payments
der **Zettel** –s,– (nm)	note
zuhören (v sep)	to listen

On the phone

to pick up the phone	(den Hörer) abnehmen
to hang up	auflegen
receiver	der Hörer
mobile phone	das Handy, das Mobiltelefon
cordless phone	das schnurlose Telefon
to dial	wählen
dialling tone	das Freizeichen
answering machine	der Anrufbeantworter
please speak after the tone	bitte sprechen Sie nach dem Tonzeichen
voice mail	die Voice-Mail
phone book	das Telefonbuch
Yellow Pages	die gelben Seiten, das Branchenverzeichnis
to be ex-directory	nicht im Telefonbuch stehen
extension number	der Apparat, der Nebenanschluss
extension 597, please	bitte verbinden Sie mich mit Apparat 597
I'll put you through	ich verbinde
it's engaged	es ist besetzt
what is the code for Munich?	wie lautet die Vorwahl von München?
phonecard	die Telefonkarte
you've got the wrong number	Sie sind falsch verbunden
I've dialled the wrong number	ich muss mich verwählt haben
I can't get through	ich komme nicht durch
would you like to leave a message?	möchten sie eine Nachricht hinterlassen?
who's calling, please?	wer ist am Apparat?
just a moment, please	einen Augenblick bitte
please hold the line	bitte bleiben Sie am Apparat
please tell him/her I called	richten Sie ihm/ihr bitte aus, dass ich angerufen habe
can I leave a message for …?	kann ich eine Nachricht für … hinterlassen?
can he/she ring me back?	kann er/sie mich zurückrufen?
who do you want to talk to?	wen möchten Sie sprechen?
there's no answer	es meldet sich niemand
my home number is …	meine Privatnummer ist …
my office number is …	meine Nummer im Büro ist …
my fax number is …	meine Faxnummer ist …
can I send a fax from here?	kann ich von hier faxen?
hello, this is Sam	hallo, hier spricht Sam
I'd like to make a phone call	ich möchte gern telefonieren
I'd like to reverse the charges	ich möchte ein R-Gespräch anmelden
we were cut off	wir sind unterbrochen worden
Is that Emma? – Speaking	Kann ich mit Emma sprechen? – Am Apparat

Key Structures

the verb **wollen** frequently means to be about to, expressing intention in the immediate future

    wir wollen die Zahlungsbilanz angehen   we are going to tackle the balance of payments.

the relative pronouns **der/die/das** introduce and link a new clause. In English they are who, which, that and what. In German relative pronouns agree in gender and number with the noun they refer to.

    Das ist mein kleiner Afrikaner,   It's the little African I'm
    den ich sponsere, der mich anruft   sponsoring, who is ringing.

ZU HAUSE

Kommen heute Abend Gäste zu uns?

Ja, Florian und Gisi.

Was machen wir am Sonntag?

Tja, ich weiß nicht. Wir könnten auf den Flohmarkt gehen.

Und was machen wir in den Osterferien?

Das weißt du doch. Du fährst mit deinem Vetter und deiner Kusine zum Snowboarden.

Aber wann machen wir dann mal Ferien in Kalifornien?

Sehr witzig! Du suchst dir immer den richtigen Augenblick für solche Geistesblitze aus.

Na ja, wenn doch alles so langweilig ist.

Angeblich soll es Eltern geben, die es fertig bringen ihre Kinder mit tollen Plänen zu motivieren. Also ...

... was machen wir in den großen Ferien?

Ich habe vor, dich zu einer amerikanischen Familie zu schicken.

Was?

Kommt nicht in Frage. Was soll ich denn bei so 'ner amerikanischen Familie? Ich hab hier klasse Spaß.

BRETECHER

Understanding the text

aber (conj)	but	
alles (pron)	everything	
also (adv)	well	
am (prep)	on	
amerikanisch (adj)	American	
angeblich (adv)	apparently, they say that …	
die **Eltern** (npl)	parents	
fahren (v*)	to go	
die **Familie** -,-n (nf)	family	
die **Ferien** (npl)	holidays, vacation	
der **Flohmarkt** -(e)s,-¨e (nm)	flea market	
der **Gast** -(e)s,-¨e (nm)	guest	
der **Geistesblitz** -es,-e (nm)	brainwave, flash of inspiration	
die **großen Ferien** (npl)	summer holidays, vacation	
heute Abend	tonight	
Kalifornien -s (nn)	California	
das **Kind** -(e)s,-er (nn)	child	
klasse (adj)	super, great	
kommen (v*)	to come	
die **Kusine** -,-n (nf)	cousin	
langweilig (adj)	boring	
machen (v)	to do	
motivieren (v)	to motivate	
na ja	well (all right)	
nach (prep)	to	
nicht in Frage kommen	to be out of the question	
die **Osterferien** (npl)	Easter holidays, vacation	
der **Plan** -(e)s,-¨e (nm)	plan	
schicken (v)	to send	
sehr (adv)	very	
das **Snowboarden** -s (nn)	snowboarding	
solcher/solche/solches (adj)	such	
der **Sonntag** -s,-e (nm)	Sunday	
tja (interj)	(yes) well	
toll (adj)	brilliant	
uns (pron)	us	
der **Vetter** -s,-n (nm)	cousin	
vorhaben (v sep*)	to intend	
was (pron)	what	
weiß (v*)	→ wissen	
wenn (conj)	if, when	
wissen (v*)	to know	
witzig (adj)	funny	
zu (prep)	to	
zu Hause	at home	

 Time off

a holiday/vacation in the mountains	Ferien/Urlaub im Gebirge
seaside holidays/vacation	Ferien/Urlaub an der See
skiing holidays/vacation	der Skiurlaub
Christmas holiday/vacation	Weihnachtsferien
Easter holiday/vacation	Osterferien
summer holidays/vacation	Sommerferien, große Ferien
half-term	Ferien in der Mitte des Trimesters, kleine Ferien
the school holidays/vacation	die Schulferien
to go on holiday/vacation	in die Ferien fahren, Ferien machen
where are you going on holiday/vacation?	wo fahrt ihr in den Ferien hin? wo macht ihr Ferien?
I had a lovely holiday/vacation in Italy	ich habe sehr schöne Ferien/einen schönen Urlaub in Italien verbracht
we are not going on holiday/vacation this year	dieses Jahr verreisen wir nicht
did you take a holiday/vacation this year?	bist du dieses Jahr verreist?
yes, I went to the mountains with the children	ja, ich war mit den Kindern in den Bergen
to go on a camping holiday/vacation	Campingurlaub machen
to take ten days' off	zehn Tage Urlaub nehmen
he's on holiday/vacation in Ireland	er ist in Irland im/in Urlaub
to have four weeks holiday/vacation with/without pay	vier Wochen bezahlten/unbezahlten Urlaub haben
she's (away) on holiday/vacation	sie ist auf Urlaub
bank/national holiday	gesetzlicher Feiertag

 Key Structures

am is the shortened form of the preposition **an** and the article **dem**.
Contractions are not used where the article is to be stressed.

was machen wir am Sonntag?	what are we doing on Sunday?
was machen wir in den Osterferien?	what are we doing at Easter?
was machen wir in den großen Ferien?	what are we doing during the summer holidays?
wann machen wir Ferien in Kalifornien?	when are we going on holiday to California?
du suchst dir immer den richtigen Augenblick aus	you choose your moment
angeblich soll es Eltern geben, die es fertig bringen, ihre Kinder mit tollen Plänen zu motivieren	apparently some parents manage to motivate their children with brilliant plans
was soll ich bei so 'ner amerikanischen Familie?	what am I supposed to do with an American family?
klasse Spaß haben	to have a great time
ich hab hier klasse Spaß	I'm having a great time here

People with paid jobs usually have **Urlaub**. Families and students have **Ferien**.

AUF INS NETZ

Nick, wir kommen zu spät.

Ich komme nicht mit, ich bin hier was auf die Spur gekommen.

QUATSCH!

Ich fahre eine halbe Stunde mit dem Bus hierher, du rufst mich nicht mal an ... du bist wirklich unmöglich.

Ich hab zufällig eine Geheimseite angeklickt, und das Passwort ... du verstehst das sowieso nicht.

Ja, denkste!

Ein Freund von mir hat in die Deutsche Bank am Marienplatz gehackt.

Ja, so Verschlüsselungen haben mich früher auch fasziniert, aber das sind Träumereien, die mich jetzt kalt lassen.

Es gibt wesentlich interessantere Dinge. Geld ist nicht das Wichtigste im Leben.

Halt!

Würdest du etwa nicht gern ein paar sechsstellige Beträge auf dein Konto überweisen?

Nein.

Was mich betrifft, rufe ich lieber die NASA-Seiten ab, als wie dein Hacker sklavisch den Millionen nachzurennen. Da kann man nur lachen!

Darf ich dein Telefon benutzen?

Ja, in der Diele.

Eine Mark bitte.

Understanding the text

aber (conj)	but
abrufen (v sep*)	to call up
anklicken (v sep)	to click on
anrufen (v sep*)	to ring, to phone
benutzen (v)	to use
der Betrag –(e)s,‥-e (nm)	sum, amount
der Bus –ses,-se (nm)	bus
darf ich ©	may I
denkste ©	that's what you think
die Diele –,-n (nf)	hall
das Ding –(e)s,-e (nn)	thing
einer Sache auf die Spur kommen	to be on to something
es gibt	there are, there is
faszinieren (v)	to fascinate
der Freund –(e)s,-e (nm)	friend
die Geheimseite –,-n (nf)	secret page
das Geld –(e)s,-er (nn)	money
hacken (v)	to hack
der Hacker –s,- (nm)	hacker
halt (interj)	stop
hierher (adv)	here
in (prep)	into
interessant (adj)	interesting
jetzt (adv)	now
komme mit (v*)	→ **mitkommen**
das Konto –s,-s (nn)	account
das Leben –s,- (nn)	life
die Mark – (nf)	mark
die Million –,-en (nf)	million
mitkommen (v sep*)	to come (along)
nachrennen (v sep*)	to chase after, to pursue
das Netz –es,-e (nn)	Internet, Net
nicht mal	not even
ein paar	a few
das Passwort –(e)s,‥-er (nn)	password
der Quatsch –(e)s (nm)	rubbish
rufe ab (v*)	→ **abrufen**
rufst an (v*)	→ **anrufen**
sechsstellig (adj)	six-figure
sein (v*)	to be
sind (v*)	→ **sein**
sklavisch (adv)	slavishly
so (adv)	like this, like that, such
sowieso (adv)	anyway
das Telefon –s,-e (nn)	phone
die Träumerei –,-en (nf)	day dream
überweisen (v*)	to transfer
unmöglich (adj)	impossible
die Verschlüsselung –,-en (nf)	coding, code
verstehen (v*)	to understand
was mich betrifft	as far as I'm concerned, for my part
wesentlich (adv)	much, considerably
das Wichtigste –n (nn)	the most important thing
wirklich (adv)	really
zufällig (adv)	by chance

⏎ Computing and the Internet

computer	der Computer, der PC
screen	der Bildschirm
keyboard	die Tastatur
(floppy) disk	die Diskette
hard disk	die Festplatte
mouse	die Maus
printer	der Drucker
to click	klicken
to enter, key in	eingeben
to click on	anklicken
cursor	der Cursor
Internet	das Internet
to have access to the Internet, to be on the Internet	Zugang zum Internet haben
to save	speichern
to back up	sichern
e-mail	die E-Mail
to receive an e-mail	eine E-Mail erhalten, bekommen
to send an e-mail	eine E-Mail verschicken, schicken
e-mail address	die E-Mail-Adresse
menu	das Menü
to dial a page	eine Internet-Seite anwählen
to delete	löschen
attachment	die Anlage
to print	ausdrucken
search engine	die Suchmaschine
file	die Datei
to have something on the computer	etwas auf/im Computer haben

The Deutsche Bank is a German bank which has many branches all over the country.
NASA (the US National Aeronautics and Space Administration) has a web-site on the worldwide web (www.nasa.gov), with a home page and many pages with information about its work, details of the space shuttle and pictures taken by the Hubble space telescope.

⏎ Key Structures

wir kommen zu spät	we'll be late
ich fahre eine halbe Stunde mit dem Bus hierher	I've been on the bus for half an hour to get here
haben mich früher fasziniert	used to fascinate me
Träumereien, die mich jetzt kalt lassen	day dreams which no longer get me all excited
würdest du etwa nicht gern	wouldn't you like to
here **etwa** means possibly and is used for stress	
rufe ich lieber die NASA-Seiten ab	I prefer calling up the NASA pages
Da kann man nur lachen!	That makes me laugh! That's a laugh!

BESORGT

Understanding the text

abends (adv)	in the evening
angerufen (v*)	→ anrufen
anrufen (v sep*)	to ring
auf der Straße	in the street
auweia (interj)	oh dear
bei (prep)	at
besorgt (adj)	worried
bist (v*)	→ sein
dass (conj)	that
erlauben (v)	to allow
finden (v*)	to find
geschlafen (v*)	→ schlafen
haben (v*)	to have
hast (v*)	→ haben
der Junge -n,-n (nm)	boy
kein (pron)	no
kriegen (v)	to get
das Mal -(e)s,-e (nn)	time
mit (prep)	with
nach Hause	home
nachspionieren (v sep)	to spy on
nächster/nächste/nächstes (adj)	next
nachts (adv)	at night
nicht mehr	any longer
oder (conj)	or
sagen (v)	to tell, to say
schlafen (v*)	to sleep
schon (adv)	already
sein (v*)	to be
sonst (adv)	otherwise, or (else)
die Straße -,-n (nf)	street
das Taxi -s,-s (nn)	taxi
trampen (v)	to hitch-hike
überfallen (v*)	to mug
überfallen werden	to get mugged
um fünf Uhr früh	at five in the morning
unmöglich (adj)	impossible
verstanden (v*)	→ verstehen
verstehen (v*)	to understand
warst (v*)	→ sein
warum (adv)	why
wecken (v)	to wake (up)
weggehen (v sep*)	to go out
weil (conj)	because
weiß, weißt (v*)	→ wissen
will (v*)	→ wollen
wissen (v*)	to know
wo (adv)	where
wollen (v*)	to want
zu Fuß gehen	to walk

▣ Emotions

happiness	das Glück
sadness	die Traurigkeit
worry	die Sorge
to worry	sich Sorgen machen
depressed	deprimiert
fear	die Angst
anger	der Ärger
love	die Liebe
jealousy	die Eifersucht
pleasure	das Vergnügen, die Freude
to laugh	lachen
to smile	lächeln
to cry	weinen
to please oneself	tun, was man will
they get on well together	sie verstehen sich gut
Anja is very moody	Anja ist sehr launisch
she's fallen in love with him	sie hat sich in ihn verliebt
he fancies Nicola	er mag Nicola
he's jealous	er ist eifersüchtig
she's jealous of Anita	sie ist auf Anita eifersüchtig
to be afraid of something	vor etwas Angst haben
to have a row, to quarrel	sich streiten
to make it up	sich wieder vertragen
don't worry about it	mach dir deswegen keine Sorgen
we were very worried, concerned	wir waren sehr besorgt
to be angry	böse sein
to get angry	böse werden
to hurt somebody's feelings	jemanden verletzen
I'm sorry	es tut mir Leid
I'm not in the mood	ich habe keine Lust mehr

▣ Key Structures

bei jdm übernachten	to stay the night at somebody's place
bei den Lorenzers hast du nicht übernachtet	you didn't stay the night at the Lorenzer's (place)
mit wem?	who with?
mit allen	with all of them, with everyone
alle waren da	they were all there, everyone was there
Was soll ich denn machen?	What am I supposed to do?
Würde dir das vielleicht passen?	How would you like that?

This use of **passen** is rather slangy and almost rude.

dass man es dir nie recht machen kann	that there's no pleasing you

DER BABYSITTER

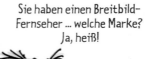

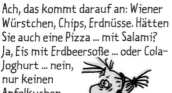

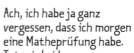

Understanding the text

also (adv)	so
der Apfelkuchen –s,– (nm)	apple-cake
babysitten (v)	to babysit
der Babysitter –s,– (nm)	babysitter
das Balg –(e)s,–̈-er ⓖ (nn)	brat
bei Ihnen	at your place
der Breitbild-Fernseher –s,– (nm)	widescreen TV
die Chips (nm pl)	crisps
das Cola –(s),–s (nn)	coke
das kommt darauf an	it depends
die Erdnuss –,–̈-e (nf)	peanut
fragen (v)	to ask
fragt (v)	→ fragen
die Freundin –,–nen (nf)	(girl)friend
ganz (adv)	completely
gehen (v*)	to go
gehst (v*)	→ gehen
guten Tag	hello
haben (v*)	to have
heiß (interj)	brilliant
heute Abend	tonight
hin und zurück	there and back
das Internet –s,–s (nn)	Internet
der Joghurt –(s),–(s) (nm)	yoghurt
der Kanal –s,–̈-e (nm)	channel
die Marke –,–n (nf)	make
die Matheprüfung –,–en (nf)	maths exam
mehr nicht?	that's all?
möchten (v)	→ mögen
mögen (v*)	to like
morgen (adv)	tomorrow
nur keinen	anything but
die Pizza –,–s (nf)	pizza
reinkriegen ⓖ (v sep)	to get
die Salami –,–s (nf)	salami
die Satellitenschüssel –,–n (nf)	satellite dish
so ein Pech	what a pity
das Taxi –s,–s (nn)	taxi, cab
trinken (v*)	to drink
tut mir Leid	I'm sorry
vergessen (v*)	to forget
das Video –s,–s (nn)	video
was wir trinken möchten?	what we would like to drink?
welcher/welche/welches (pron)	which
wenn es nichts Gutes gibt	if there's nothing good on
die Wiener Würstchen (nn pl)	sausages
wirklich (adv)	really
wollen (v*)	to want
zahlen (v)	to pay

apple	der Apfel
banana	die Banane
cherry	die Kirsche
peach	der Pfirsich
pear	die Birne
plum	die Pflaume
raspberry	die Himbeere
strawberry	die Erdbeere
orange	die Orange
lemon	die Zitrone
grape	die Weintraube
Brussels sprouts	der Rosenkohl (sing)
cauliflower	der Blumenkohl
cabbage	der Kohl
carrot	die Karotte, die Möhre
cucumber	die Gurke
lettuce	der Salat
pea	die Erbse
a pepper	eine Paprikaschote
potato	die Kartoffel
onion	die Zwiebel
garlic	der Knoblauch
beef	das Rindfleisch
roast beef	der Rinderbraten
chicken	das Huhn
roast chicken	das Brathähnchen
fish	der Fisch
leg of lamb	die Lammkeule
pork	das Schweinefleisch
a coffee with milk	ein Kaffee mit Milch
a black coffee	ein Kaffee ohne Milch
fruit juice	der Fruchtsaft
beer	das Bier
lemonade	die Limonade
water	das Wasser
mineral water	das Mineralwasser
sparkling/still mineral water	Mineralwasser mit Kohlensäure/ ohne Kohlensäure
wine	der Wein
tea	der Tee
bread	das Brot
cake	der Kuchen
cold meats	der Aufschnitt (sing)
cheese	der Käse
butter	die Butter
sugar	der Zucker
salt	das Salz
pasta	Nudeln (nf pl)
rice	der Reis
soup	die Suppe
oil	das Öl
vinegar	der Essig

Key Structures

fragen, ob — to ask if
When introducing an indirect question **ob** is translated with if.
Sie fragt, ob du heute Abend babysitten willst. She's asking if you'd like to babysit tonight.

wie viele Kanäle kriegen Sie rein? how many channels can you get?
the verb **reinkriegen** is colloquial for **hereinbekommen**

komme ich bei Ihnen ins Internet? can I get on the Internet at your place?

hätten Sie auch eine Pizza? do you have pizza too?
hätte is the past subjunctive of **haben**. The subjunctive is frequently used in requests and questions, to sound more polite.

ich hätte gern deine Mutter gesprochen could I speak to your mother?, I would like to speak to your mother

EIN GEBURTSTAGSGESCHENK

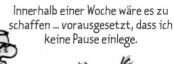

Understanding the text

aufführen (v sep)	to perform	
aufnehmen (v sep*)	to record	
bestimmt (adv)	certainly, definitely	
der **Comicstrip –s,–s** (nm)	comic strip	
einfach (adv)	simply	
etwas (pron)	something	
ewig dauern ⓒ	to take ages, for ever	
filmen (v)	to film	
ganz bestimmt	for certain	
der **Geburtstag –(e)s,–e** (nm)	birthday	
das **Geburtstagsgeschenk –(e)s,–e** (nn)	birthday present	
die **Geburtstagskarte –,–n** (nf)	birthday card	
die **Geschichte –,–n** (nf)	story	
groß (adj)	big, large	
die **Hauptperson –,–en** (nf)	most important person, star	
innerhalb (prep)	within	
irgendwas Nettes	something nice	
ja gut	well, yes	
die **Kassette –,–n** (nf)	cassette, tape	
keine Pause einlegen	to have no break	
klein (adj)	small	
das **Leben –s,–** (nn)	life	
das **Lied –(e)s,–er** (nn)	song	
machen (v)	to do	
der **Mann –(e)s,–̈er** (nm)	husband	
meinen (v)	to think	
meinst du nicht?	don't you think (so)?	
mit (prep)	with	
morgen (adv)	tomorrow	
die **Mutter –,–̈** (nf)	mother	
sagen (v)	to say	
schaffen (v)	to manage	
schenken (v)	to give	
schicken (v)	to send	
der **Schnitt –(e)s** (nm)	cutting	
schreiben (v*)	to write	
sich überlegen (v)	to think (about)	
sicherlich (adv)	surely	
Spaß machen	to be fun	
der **Stammbaum –(e)s,–̈e** (nm)	family tree	
der **Stiefbruder –s,–̈** (nm)	stepbrother	
die **Videokamera –,–s** (nf)	video camera	
vielleicht (adv)	perhaps	
vorausgesetzt, dass	provided that	
will (v*)	→ **wollen**	
wollen (v*)	to want	
die **Zeichnung –,–en** (nf)	drawing	
das **Zubehör –s** (nn)	equipment	
zwischen (prep)	between	

⊡ Art and Literature

painting	(activity) **die Malerei;** (picture) **das Gemälde**
sculpture	(activity) **die Bildhauerei;**
	(piece of work) **die Skulptur, die Plastik**
engraving	**der Stich**
drawing	**die Zeichnung**
music	**die Musik**
theatre	**das Theater**
cinema	**das Kino**
ballet	**das Ballett**
dance	**der Tanz**
dancing	**das Tanzen**
literature	**die Literatur**
architecture	**die Architektur**
art gallery	**die Kunstgalerie**
art	**die Kunst**
museum	**das Museum**
concert hall	**die Konzerthalle**
poetry	**die Dichtung**
painter	**der Maler**
sculptor	**der Bildhauer**
poet	**der Dichter**
works of art	**Kunstwerke** (pl)
art and craft	**das Kunthandwerk, das Kunstgewerbe**
exhibition	**die Ausstellung**
composer	**der Komponist**
to go to the opera	**in die Oper gehen**
contemporary music	**zeitgenössische Musik**
fine arts	**die bildenden Künste** (pl)
artist	**der Künstler/die Künstlerin**
graphic art	**die Grafik**
performance (of a play)	**die Aufführung**
director	**der Regisseur**
author	**der Autor/die Autorin, der**
	Schriftsteller/die Schriftstellerin
paperback	**das Taschenbuch**

⊡ Key Structures

jemandem etw zum Geburtstag schenken	to give somebody a birthday present, to give somebody something for their birthday
was ich machen könnte	what I could do
ich könnte eine Kassette aufnehmen	I could record a cassette
mit Liedern aus ihrer Zeit	with songs from her time, from her day
Das würde ihr bestimmt Spaß machen, meinst du nicht?	That would be fun for her, wouldn't it, don't you think (so)?
wäre es zu schaffen	it could be done, I might manage it
the past subjunctive (**wäre**) is often used in conversation to tone down a suggestion	
sie hat morgen Geburtstag	her birthday is tomorrow
das macht viel zu viel Arbeit	that's much ttoo much bother

The Earth

Understanding the text

aber (conj)	but
abschreiben (v sep*)	to crib, to copy
alles (pron)	everything
die **Arbeit** –,–en (nf)	paper
beantworten (v)	to answer
dabei (adv)	although
das mag ja wahr sein	that might well be true
die **Eins** –,–en (nf)	one
die **Entwicklung** –,–en (nf)	development
die **Erschließung** –,–en (nf)	development, tapping
erster/erste/erstes (adj)	first
die **Fehlentscheidung** –,–en (nf)	wrong decision
die **Frage** –,–n (nf)	question
geben (v*)	to give
geschrieben (v*)	→ schreiben
kurz (adv)	quickly
neu (adj)	new
der **Regenwald** –(e)s,¨–er (nm)	rainforest
die **Ressource** –,–n (nf)	resource
schreiben (v*)	to write
die **Sechs** –,–en (nf)	six
tropisch (adj)	tropical
ungerecht (adj)	unfair
Zentralasien –s (nn)	Central Asia
zweiter/zweite/zweites (adj)	second

 Key Structures

Mario Müller hat eine Eins geschrieben	Mario Müller got an A
das ist ungerecht	it's unfair
mir haben Sie eine Sechs gegeben	you gave me an E

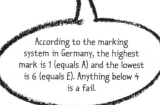

According to the marking system in Germany, the highest mark is 1 (equals A) and the lowest is 6 (equals E). Anything below 4 is a fail.

⊞ The Earth

earth	die Erde
sky	der Himmel
sea	das Meer, die See
star	der Stern
sun	die Sonne
moon	der Mond
ocean	der Ozean
continent	der Kontinent, der Erdteil
the continents of Europe, Asia, Africa	die Erdteile Europa, Asien, Afrika
the Continent	das europäische Festland, der Kontinent
mountain	der Berg
river	der Fluss
the Northern/Southern hemisphere	die nördliche/südliche Halbkugel/Hemisphäre
the Arctic/Antarctic circle	der nördliche/südliche Polarkreis
equator	der Äquator
at the seaside	am Meer
a seaside resort	ein Ferienort am Meer, an der See
the tide is in/out	es ist Flut/Ebbe
when the tide is in/out	bei Flut/Ebbe
in the mountains	in den Bergen, im Gebirge
snow	der Schnee
it's snowing	es schneit
a torrent	ein reißender Strom
ski resort	der Skiurlaubsort
weather	das Wetter
thunder	der Donner
lightning	der Blitz
frost	der Frost
ice	das Eis
to fall through the ice	auf dem Eis einbrechen
fog	der Nebel
what's the weather like?	wie ist das Wetter?
it's fine today	heute haben wir schönes Wetter
the forecast for tomorrow is rain	laut Wettervorhersage wird es morgen regnen

47

KARMA

Understanding the text

alles (pron)	everything
am besten	best
auch (adv)	also
aufräumen (v sep)	to tidy up
die Batterie –,–n (nf)	battery
bedeuten (v)	to mean
die Beruhigungspille –,–n (nf)	tranquillizer, sedative (pill)
darum (adv)	that's why
dass (conj)	that
einlegen (v sep)	to put in, to insert
einmal (adv)	one day, some day
entscheidend (adj)	decisive
es gibt	there is, there are
früherer/frühere/früheres (adj)	earlier, previous
für (prep)	for
gegenwärtig (adj)	present
heiß (interj)	great
herrlich (adj)	magnificent
hin und wieder	now and again
in (prep)	in
ist (v*)	→ sein
jemanden nerven	to get on somebody's nerves
das Karma –s (nn)	karma
das Leben –s,– (nn)	life
leicht (adv)	easily
machen (v)	to do
man (pron)	one, you
oder (conj)	or
der Palast –(e)s,¨–e (nm)	palace
die Putzfrau –,–en (nf)	cleaner, charwoman
der Quatsch –es ⑤ (nm)	rubbish

sagen (v)	to say
das Schicksal –s, –e (nn)	destiny, fate
Schluss jetzt!	that'll do! stop it!
sein (v*)	to be
so (adv)	such
so wenig wie möglich	as little as possible
sofort (adv)	at once, immediately
umgekehrt (adv)	the other way round
verfluchen (v)	to curse
warum (adv)	why
was (pron)	what
wenn (conj)	if
werden (v*)	to become
wirklich (adv)	really
wohnen (v)	to live
das Zimmer –s,– (nn)	room
zukünftig (adj)	future
zum Beispiel	for example

⊡ Key Structures

Beruhigungspillen schlucken (literally to swallow pills) is a jokey way of saying that someone is taking a lot of tranquillizers without thinking much about it.

Das ist doch nicht so schwer, oder?	It can't be that hard, can it?
dann könntest du vielleicht	
einmal … wohnen	you might one day live …
oder ich könnte auch … werden	or I might also become …

können corresponds to can or is able to. But it also expresses possibility. The past subjunctive **(könnte)** expresses more remote possibility.

⊡ Health

illness, disease	**die Krankheit**
infectious	**ansteckend**
to be ill	**krank sein**
to be well	**gesund sein**
I'm very well, thank you	**danke, es geht mir gut**
he is not well	**ihm geht es nicht gut**
get well soon!	**gute Besserung!**
I have a headache	**ich habe Kopfschmerzen/Kopfweh**
does it hurt?	**tut es weh?**
that hurts!	**das tut weh!**
my arm hurts	**der Arm tut mir weh**
did you hurt yourself?	**hast du dir wehgetan?**
I sprained my ankle	**ich habe mir den Fuß verstaucht**
she broke her arm	**sie hat sich den Arm gebrochen**
I have toothache	**ich habe Zahnschmerzen**
to have an operation	**operiert werden**
flu	**die Grippe**
cold	**der Schnupfen**
food poisoning	**die Lebensmittelvergiftung**
he has diarrhoea/earache	**er hat Durchfall/Ohrenschmerzen**
she feels dizzy	**ihr ist schwindlig**
to be diabetic	**zuckerkrank sein**
she is pregnant	**sie ist schwanger**
spot, pimple	**der Pickel**
hayfever	**der Heuschnupfen**
asthma	**das Asthma**
to be allergic to penicillin	**gegen Penizillin allergisch sein**
she has been sick (= vomited)	**sie hat sich übergeben**
I feel sick	**mir ist schlecht**
to have a temperature	**Fieber haben**
he has been stung/bitten	**er ist gestochen/gebissen worden**
mosquito bite	**der Mückenstich**

Understanding the text

anderer/andere/anderes (adj)	other
anhaben (v sep*)	to wear, to have on
anziehen (v sep*)	to dress
auch (adv)	too, also
auf (prep)	on
aussehen (v sep*)	to look
bin (v*)	→ sein
dass (conj)	that
dein (adj)	your
der/die/das andere (pron)	the other one
eben (adv)	just
das Foto –s,–s (nn)	photo
furchtbar (adj)	terrible
genau (adv)	exactly
gleich (adj)	same
ich auch	me too
die Jacke –,–n (nf)	jacket
jedenfalls (adv)	in any case, anyway
machen (v)	to do
das Mädchen –s,– (nn)	girl
meinen (v)	to think
müssen (v*)	must
noch mal = noch einmal	again
der Rollkragenpulli –s,–s (nm)	polo neck
der Schnappschuss –es,¨–e (nm)	snapshot
seh aus (v*)	→ aussehen
sein (v*)	to be
vor uns	in front of us
wenn (conj)	when, if
wie ich	as me
wirklich (adv)	really
das Zeug –s ⓖ (nn)	clothes, stuff

Clothes

belt	der Gürtel
shirt	das Hemd
blouse	die Bluse
dress	das Kleid
dressing gown	der Morgenrock
tights	die Strumpfhose (nf sing)
gloves	die Handschuhe (nm pl)
jeans	die Jeans (nf sing or pl)
swimming costume	der Badeanzug
trunks	die Badehose (nf sing)
coat	der Mantel
trousers	die Hose (nf), die Hosen (pl)
a pair of trousers	eine Hose
jacket	die Jacke
underwear	die Unterwäsche
bra	der Büstenhalter
knickers	der Schlüpfer (nm sing)
underpants	die Unterhose (nf sing)
boxer shorts	die Boxershort (nf sing)
raincoat	der Regenmantel
shoe	der Schuh
a pair of shoes	ein Paar Schuhe
boots	die Stiefel (nm pl)
cap	die Kappe, die Mütze
sweater	der Pullover
skirt	der Rock
top	das Top
T-shirt	das T-Shirt
to wear jeans	Jeans anhaben, tragen
to get dressed	sich anziehen
to put on a dress	ein Kleid anziehen
to be well dressed	gut gekleidet sein
I've got nothing to wear	ich habe nichts anzuziehen
the dress doesn't suit her	das Kleid steht ihr nicht

Key Structures

das bin ich überhaupt nicht	that's definitely not me
das bin ich nie	that's never me, no way that's me
das muss ein Mädchen sein, die vor uns war	that must be a girl who was before us

Although the relative pronouns **der/die/das** always agree in gender and number with the noun they refer back to, **das Mädchen** is treated as feminine.

kanns is colloquial for **kann es**. There are a number of such contractions in which the last letter of the pronoun **es** is added to the previous word:

ich kanns nicht ausstehen	I can't stand it
wie gehts? (wie geht es?)	how are you?

was andres anziehen is colloquial for e**twas anderes anziehen**   wear something else

HITPARADE

Understanding the text

ach (interj)	oh	
ah (interj)	oh, ah	
also (adv)	well	
alt (adj)	old	
arm (adj)	poor	
bitte (adv)	please	
das Buch –(e)s,¨–er (nn)	book	
dick (adj)	big	
du bists = du bist es	it's you	
furchtbar (adj)	awful	
ganz (adv)	very, really	
der Garten –s,¨– (nm)	garden	
geben (v*)	to give	
gib (v*)	→ geben	
griechisch (adj)	Greek	
haben (v*)	to have	
hallo (interj)	hi, hello	
die Hitparade –,–n (nf)	hit parade, Top of the Pops	
in (prep)	in	
jetzt (adv)	now	
klein (adj)	little	
die Küche –,–n (nf)	kitchen	
der Kuss –es,¨–e (nm)	kiss	
der Liebling –s,–e (nm)	darling	
liegen lassen (v*)	to leave (behind)	
der Macker –s,– ⓖ (nm)	mate	
die Mutti –,–s (nf)	mum	
ne (adv)	no	
nebenbei (adv)	vaguely	
nur so	only	
die Oma –,–s (nf)	granny	
die Ruhe – (nf)	silence	
sehen (v*)	to watch	
sich vorstellen (v sep*)	to imagine	
stell dir vor	imagine	
stinklangweilig ⓖ (adj)	deadly boring	
der Vater –s,¨– (nm)	father	

⬇ Television

television	das Fernsehen
television (set)	der Fernseher
programme	die Sendung
news	die Nachrichten
weather forecast	der Wetterbericht
film	der Spielfilm
sport	die Sportsendung
adverts	die Werbung
documentary	der Dokumentarfilm
talk show	die Talkshow
thriller	der Krimi
review	die Kritik
game show	die Gameshow
TV series	die Fernsehserie
soap opera	die Seifenoper
children's programme	die Kindersendung
sitcom	die Situationskomödie
aerial	die Antenne
channel	der Kanal
remote control	die Fernbedienung
digital TV	das Digitalfernsehen
to watch TV	fernsehen
I like to watch TV	ich sehe gern fern
the programme is on at 8 p.m.	die Sendung läuft um 20 Uhr
what's on TV today?	was läuft heute im Fernsehen?
is there anything on television?	gibts was im Fernsehen?
there's a cartoon on this afternoon	heute Nachmittag läuft ein Zeichentrickfilm
the presenter is very good	der Moderator/die Moderatorin ist sehr gut
did you watch the documentary about lions?	hast du den Dokumentarfilm über Löwen gesehen?
that series was filmed in Munich	die Serie ist in München verfilmt worden
to turn the TV on/off	den Fernseher einschalten/ausschalten
to switch over to another programme	auf ein anderes Programm umschalten
can you switch over?	kannst du umschalten?
to switch to TV (from video)	ins Fernsehprogramm schalten
to choose a channel	einen Kanal wählen

⬇ Key Structures

nix Besonderes ⓖ **= nichts Besonderes**	nothing special
Ruhe!	quiet! or silence!
jemanden um Ruhe bitten	to ask somebody to be quiet
um Ruhe bitten	to ask for silence
vor jemandem Ruhe haben	not be bothered by somebody
ich möchte mal meine Ruhe haben	I'd like to have some peace and quiet

ZUKUNFTSPLÄNE

Understanding the text

abwerten (v sep)	to devalue
also (adv)	well
am meisten	most
aufgeben (v sep*)	to give up
die Ausbildung -,-en (nf)	education
beim Anblick von	at the sight of
der Beruf -(e)s,-e (nm)	profession
das Blut -(e)s (nn)	blood
die Chirurgin -,-nen (nf)	surgeon
das Einzige	the only thing
ein Haufen Geld	a lot of money, loads of money
die Fehlkalkulation -,-en (nf)	miscalculation, mistake
feststehen (v sep*)	to be certain
für (prep)	for
furchtbar (adj)	terrible
gut (adj)	good
haben (v*)	to have
hast (v*)	→ haben
heiraten (v)	to marry
homöopathisch (adj)	homeopathic
hübsch (adj)	pretty
immer mehr	more and more
inzwischen (adv)	by now
kein (adj)	no
die Literatur - (nf)	literature
machen (v)	to do, to make
das Mädchen -s,- (nn)	girl
mein (adj)	my
mich (pron)	me
mir wird schlecht	I feel sick
muss (v*)	→ müssen
müssen (v*)	to have to
nachdenken (v sep*)	to think about
nachgedacht (v*)	→ nachdenken
der Notar -s,-e (nm)	notary
das Problem -s,-e (nn)	problem
rausschmeißen (v sep*)	to chuck, to ditch
sagen (v)	to say
schon wieder	already
sowieso (adv)	anyway
später einmal	one day (in the future)
das Studium -s,-ien (nn)	studies
verdienen (v)	to earn
was (pron)	that
wild auf etwas sein ©	to be mad on something
willst (v*)	→ wollen
wirklich (adv)	really
wollen (v*)	to want
der Zukunftsplan -(e)s,¨-e (nm)	future plan, plan for the future
zum Beispiel	for example

Work

accountant	der Buchhalter/die Buchhalterin
actor	der Schauspieler/die Schauspielerin
bank clerk	der/die Bankangestellte
boss	der Chef/die Chefin
businessman/businesswoman	der Geschäftsmann/die Geschäftsfrau
caretaker	der Hausmeister/die Hausmeisterin
dentist	der Zahnarzt/die Zahnärztin
driver	der Fahrer/die Fahrerin
engineer	der Ingenier/die Ingenieurin, (service engineer) der Techniker/die Technikerin
farmer	der Landwirt /die Landwirtin
fire officer	der Feuerwehrmann
hairdresser	der Friseur/die Friseuse
journalist	der Journalist/die Journalistin
mechanic	der Mechaniker/die Mechanikerin
musician	der Musiker/die Musikerin
nurse	der Krankenpfleger/die Krankenschwester
petrol-pump attendant	der Tankwart/die Tankwärtin
pilot	der Pilot/die Pilotin
plumber	der Installateur, der Klempner
postman/postwoman	der Postbote/die Postbotin
programmer	der Programmierer/die Programmiererin
shopkeeper	der Ladenbesitzer/die Ladenbesitzerin
teacher	der Lehrer/die Lehrerin
worker	der Arbeiter/die Arbeiterin
employee	der/die Angestellte
vet	der Tierarzt/die Tierärztin
waiter/waitress	der Kellner/die Kellnerin
writer	der Autor/die Autorin
salary	das Gehalt
working hours	die Arbeitszeit (nf sing)
to earn	verdienen
to be under contract to do something	vertraglich verpflichtet sein, etwas zu tun
to work at the hairdresser's	beim Friseur arbeiten
freelance	freiberuflich
to work part-time	Teilzeit arbeiten
a full-time job	eine Ganztagsstelle

Key Structures

Terms of endearment all translate more or less the same: my darling, love, sweety. The ending -chen is often added to such words.

mein Schätzchen
mein Herzchen
meine Süße
mein Liebling
mein Schatz

ich werde Chirurgin	I'll be a surgeon

In sentences describing a person's profession the article (a/an) is not translated:

ihre Mutter ist Ärztin	her mother is a doctor

But if an adjective describes the profession, the article is used:

sein Vater ist ein guter Chirurg	his father is a good surgeon
dieser Beruf wird immer mehr abgewertet	that profession is being devalued more and more, that profession's worth less and less all the time

TRAUMFRAU

Understanding the text

anfangen (v sep*)	to begin
der **Bauch** –(e)s, ¨–e (nm)	stomach, tummy
das **Berufsleben** –s (nn)	professional life
der **Busen** –s,– (nm)	breasts, bosom
danach (adv)	afterwards
dann (adv)	then
einplanen (v sep)	to plan, to allow for
erfolgreich (adj)	successful
das **Familienleben** –s (nn)	family life
für (prep)	for
das **Gefühlsleben** –s (nn)	emotional life
im Jahr	in (the year)
die **Karriere** –,–n (nf)	career
das **Kind** –(e)s,–er (nn)	child
leben (v)	to live
machen (v)	to do
die **Nasenkorrektur** –,–en (nf)	nose job
der **Oberschenkel** –s,– (nm)	thigh
operieren (v)	to operate on
plane ein (v)	→ einplanen
sich um etwas kümmern	to take care of something
die **Traumfrau** –,–en (nf)	dream woman
was (pron)	what
weiß (v*)	→ wissen
weiß ich nicht	I don't know
wissen (v*)	to know
zwischen (prep)	between

➡ Key Structures

sich operieren lassen	to have an operation, to have surgery
sich am Busen kosmetisch operieren lassen	to have cosmetic breast surgery
sich die Oberschenkel machen lassen	to have one's thighs done
kriege ich drei Kinder	I'll have three children
ich lasse mir den Bauch straffen	I'll/I'm going to have a stomach lift
ein erfolgreiches Berufs-, Familien- und Gefühlsleben	a successful professional, family and emotional life

The hyphen in **Berufs-** and **Familien-** stands for **leben**, to save the word having to appear three times.

lasse ich mich von Kopf bis Fuß liften	I'll/I'm going to have everything lifted (literally: I'll/I'm going to be lifted from head to foot)

➡ The Human Body

neck	der Hals
body	der Körper
chest	die Brust
arm	der Arm
leg	das Bein
bottom	der Hintern
waist	die Taille
hip	die Hüfte
shoulder	die Schulter
knee	das Knie
elbow	der Ellbogen
hand	die Hand
ankle	der Knöchel
foot	der Fuß
toe	der Zeh
finger	der Finger
heart	das Herz
brain	das Gehirn
lung	die Lunge
stomach	der Magen, der Bauch
ear	das Ohr
eye	das Auge
green eyes	grüne Augen
eyebrow	die Augenbraue
eyelash	die Augenwimper
eyelid	das Augenlid
cheek	die Backe
lip	die Lippe

she has got red lips	sie hat rote Lippen
hair	die Haare (pl)
to have long/short hair	lange/kurze Haare haben
a hair	ein Haar
to have a stomach-ache	Magenschmerzen haben
he's got a headache	er hat Kopfschmerzen/Kopfweh
I go to the gym to keep fit	ich gehe ins Fitnesscenter, um fit zu bleiben/sein
she has lost weight	sie hat abgenommen
he has put on weight	er hat zugenommen
I sprained my wrist	ich habe mir das Handgelenk verstaucht
to have an operation	operiert werden

Understanding the text

abholen (v sep)	to collect, to pick up
absetzen (v sep)	to drop off
am = an dem (prep)	at
am See	by the lake
auf dem Rückweg	on the/his way back
auf jeden Fall	in any case
das Barbecue –(s),–s (nn)	barbecue
bestimmt (adv)	certainly, definitely
bis ins = bis in das	to the
das Café –s,–s (nn)	café
dann (adv)	then
dass (conj)	that
das Dorf –(e)s,¨–er (nn)	village
du (pron)	you
euch (pron)	you
fahre hin (v*)	→ hinfahren
fragen (v)	to ask
der Freund –(e)s,–e (nm)	boyfriend
für den Notfall	just in case, in case of emergency
glauben (v)	to think
heute Abend	tonight
hinfahren (v sep*)	to drive there
hole ab (v)	→ abholen
ich (pron)	I
ihr (pron)	her
kann (v*)	→ können
kommt nicht in Frage	that's out of the question
können (v*)	can (to be able)
leicht (adv)	easily
die List –,–en (nf)	(cunning) trick
man kann	one can, you can

die Mark – (nf)	mark
mit List und Tücke	by cunning and trickery
mitnehmen (v sep*)	to give a lift to
mitnimmt (v*)	→ mitnehmen
die Mutter –,¨– (nf)	mother
die Mutti –,–s (nf)	mum
nächster/nächste/nächstes (adj)	nearest, next
nehmen (v*)	to take
nein (adv)	no
okay (interj)	OK
per Anhalter fahren	to hitch-hike
das Pokerspiel –s,–e (nn)	game of poker
der See –s,–n (nm)	lake
setzt ab (v)	→ absetzen
der Spaß –es,¨–e (nm)	fun
um Punkt 23 Uhr	at exactly 11 o'clock
und (conj)	and
und da	and there
uns (pron)	us
der Vater –s,¨– (nm)	father
vereinbaren (v)	to arrange
von (prep)	from
von dir	from you
warum (adv)	why
wir könnten	we could
zu Fuß gehen	to walk
zurück (adv)	back
zurückfahren (v sep*)	to drive back
zurückfährt (v*)	→ zurückfahren

Key Structures

jemanden mitnehmen	to give somebody a lift
sie nehmen uns mit	they are giving us a lift
jemanden nach Hause bringen	to take somebody home
jemanden fragen, ob er uns nach Hause bringt	ask somebody if they'd take us home
am schnellsten	fastest

am schnellsten is the superlative of the adverb **schnell**

the superlative of adverbs is formed:

am + adverb + –sten/–esten

am langsamsten	slowest
er ist am intelligentesten	he's the most intelligent

Transport

car	das Auto, der Wagen
bus	der Bus
tram	die Straßenbahn
underground	die U-Bahn
to go by underground	mit der U-Bahn fahren
train	der Zug
to go by train	mit der Bahn fahren
local train	die S-Bahn
intercity train	der Intercityzug, der IC
compartment	das Abteil
boat	das Schiff
plane	das Flugzeug
station	der Bahnhof
airport	der Flughafen
bus stop	die Bushaltestelle
bicycle	das Fahrrad, das Rad
moped	das Moped
motorcycle	das Motorrad
I'll drive there	ich fahre mit dem Auto dahin
this train goes to Berlin	dieser Zug geht nach Berlin
the train leaves from platform 2	der Zug fährt von Gleis 2 ab
what time is the next train/flight to …?	wann geht der nächste Zug/Flug nach …?
where do I get the bus for …?	wo fährt der Bus nach … ab?
to take a taxi	ein Taxi nehmen
to change for Munich	nach München umsteigen
to book a seat	einen Platz reservieren

FITNESSTRAINING

Understanding the text

als (conj)	when
also gut	well
anhaben (v sep*)	to wear
anrufen (v sep*)	to call
auf etwas antworten	to reply to something, to say something in reply
außer Betrieb sein	to be out of order
das Babysitting –s (nn)	baby-sitting
bezahlen (v)	to pay (for)
die Dame –,–n (nf)	lady
die Treppe runterrasen	to rush downstairs
es mit etwas übertreiben	to go over the top with something
fahre runter (v*)	→ runterfahren
der Fahrstuhl –(e)s,¨-e (nm)	lift
die Fitness – (nf)	fitness
das Fitnesstraining –s (nn)	fitness training, keeping fit
die Frau –,–en (nf)	woman
geh die Treppe hoch!	walk up(stairs)!
gehen (v*)	to walk, to go
gestern (adv)	yesterday
gleich (adv)	immediately
habe an (v*)	→ anhaben
hochgehen (v sep*)	to walk up, to go up
holen (v)	to fetch, to get
irre (adv)	terribly
der Joggingschuh –(e)s,–e (nm)	jogging/running shoe
kaputt (adj)	broken(–down)
kennen (v*)	to know
kennst (v*)	→ kennen
das Kind –(e)s,–er (nn)	kid, child
manche Leute	some people
nach oben	upstairs
ohne (prep)	without
der Rechtsanwalt –(e)s,¨-e (nm)	lawyer
reparieren (v)	to repair
die Riesendachterrassenwohnung –,–en (nf)	huge roof-terrace flat
runterfahren (v sep*)	to go down
runterrasen ⓖ (v sep)	to rush down
sagen (v)	to tell
selbst (pron)	herself
sich fit halten	to keep fit
sobald (conj)	as soon as
der Spielplatz –es,¨-e (nm)	playground
der Stock –(e)s (nm)	floor
die Stunde –,–n (nf)	hour
das Treppensteigen –s (nn)	climbing stairs
unten (adv)	downstairs
weißt (v*)	→ wissen
wirklich (adv)	really
wissen (v*)	to know
wo sonst	where else
zentnerschwer (adj)	weighing a ton, that weighs a ton
zu Fuß	on foot
zurückkam (v*)	→ zurückkommen
zurückkommen (v sep*)	to come back

Sport

sport	der Sport
do you do any sports?	treiben Sie/treibst du Sport?
do you go jogging?	gehst du joggen?
she goes jogging every morning	sie joggt jeden Morgen
I play rugby/hockey/tennis	ich spiele Rugby/Hockey/Tennis
I want to do aerobics	ich will Aerobic machen
do you want to play badminton?	willst du Federball spielen?
to swim	schwimmen
I (don't) like swimming	ich gehe (nicht) gern schwimmen
football/soccer	der Fußball
to play football	Fußball spielen
he plays football	er spielt Fußball
(playing) football is fun	Fußballspielen/Fußball macht Spaß
tennis	das Tennis
badminton	der Federball, das Badminton
the Olympics/Olympic Games	die Olympischen Spiele, die Olympiade
swimming	das Schwimmen
running	das Laufen
athletics	die Leichtathletik
athletic	sportlich
I like skiing	ich laufe gern Ski
he skis well/he's a good skier	er läuft gut Ski
cross-country skiing	der Langlauf
water skiing	das Wasserskilaufen
skateboarding	Skateboard fahren
roller skating	das Rollschuhlaufen
to roller skate	Rollschuh laufen
rollerblades	die Inliner (npl)
horse riding	das Reiten
to cycle	Rad fahren
cycling	das Radfahren

Key Structures

Gestern war ich zum Babysitten bei einer Frau	yesterday I baby-sat for a woman
ich habe die Dame angerufen	I rang the lady up
the verb **haben** is used with another verb to form past tenses.	
Weißt du, was sie darauf geantwortet hat?	Do you know what she said in reply?
Treppensteigen hält fit!	Climbing the stairs keeps you fit!
das ist kein Honigschlecken!	(literally: it's not like lapping up honey) it's no picnic!
Nur keine Aufregung!	Don't get excited! Keep your cool!

WER HÖRT MIT?

Understanding the text

aber (conj)	but
alles (pron)	everything
antworten (v)	to answer, to reply
auch (adv)	too
aufstehen (v sep*)	to get up
die B-Sprache –,-n (nf)	secret language (see Note)
das Büro –s,-s (nn)	office, study
da (adv)	there
eigentlich (adv)	actually
einen Moment mal	wait a moment, hang on a sec
fragen (v)	to ask
gehen (v*)	to go
genauso (adv)	just the same
glauben (v)	to believe, to think
hört mit (v*)	→ mithören
irgendwas = irgendetwas (pron)	something
ist (v*)	→ sein
jemand (pron)	somebody, someone
jetzt (adv)	now
kann (v*)	→ können
kommst zurecht (v*)	→ zurechtkommen
können (v)	to be able to (can)
kriegen (v)	to get
die Mark – (nf)	mark
Mist (interj)	damn
mit (prep)	with
mithören (v sep*)	to listen in
mittelmäßig (adv)	average
monatlich (adv)	monthly
die Mutter –,-̈ (nf)	mother
reden (v)	to talk
sagen (v)	to say
sein (v*)	to be
setzt sich hin (v)	→ sich hinsetzen
sich hinsetzen (v sep)	to sit down
steht auf (v*)	→ aufstehen
das Taschengeld –(e)s,-er (nn)	pocket money
der Vater –s,-̈ (nm)	father
wart mal	hang on
warten (v)	to wait
weiß (v*)	→ wissen
wieder (adv)	again
will (v*)	→ wollen
wissen (v*)	to know
wollen (v*)	to want
zurechtkommen (v sep*)	to get on

Economy

the economic situation	**die Wirtschaftslage**
growth	**das Wachstum**
foreign trade	**der Außenhandel**
competition	**die Konkurrenz**
consumption	**der Verbrauch**
consumer	**der Verbraucher/die Verbraucherin**
gross income	**das Bruttoeinkommen**
the public sector	**der öffentliche/staatliche Sektor**
the private sector	**die Privatwirtschaft**
balance of payments	**die Zahlungsbilanz**
balance of trade	**die Handelsbilanz**
import	**der Import**
export	**der Export**
subsidy	**die Subvention**
share	(part of company's capital) **die Aktie**; (part-ownership of property) **der Anteil/Geschäftsanteil**
shareholder	**der Aktionär/die Aktionärin**
stock exchange	**die Börse**
industry	**die Industrie**
tourism	**der Tourismus, der Fremdenverkehr**
unemployment	**die Arbeitslosigkeit**
unemployment benefit	**das Arbeitslosengeld**
business	**die Geschäfte** (pl)
business is bad/good	**die Geschäfte gehen schlecht/gut**
company	**die Gesellschaft, das Unternehmen**
firm	**die Firma**
supply and demand	**(das) Angebot und (die) Nachfrage**
service industry	**der Dienstleistungsbetrieb**
financial year	**das Geschäftsjahr**
annual turnover	**der Jahresumsatz**
tax bracket	**die Steuergruppe**
mortgage	**die Hypothek**
income tax	**die Einkommenssteuer**
price	**der Preis**
wholesale price	**der Großhandelspreis**
retail price	**der Einzelhandelspreis, der Verkaufspreis**

> **B-Sprache** is a slang form of secret language mainly spoken by schoolchildren. It is formed by adding a b after every vowel and repeating the vowel after the b. In this way **groß** becomes groboß, **furchtbar** becomes fuburchtbabar, **Anteil** becomes Abanteibeil, **nicht** becomes nibicht, and **Schönheit** becomes Schöbönheibeit.

Key Structures

es macht mich wahnsinnig	it drives me mad
tut so, als interessiere sie nichts	pretends she isn't interested in anything
das nervt	it gets on my nerves
Frag mich was	Ask me something/some questions
jemandem eine Frage stellen	to ask somebody a question/to put a question to somebody

LITERATUR

Understanding the text

abgesehen davon, dass	apart from the fact that
ausflippen ⓢ (v sep)	to go mad
aussehen (v sep*)	to look
aussieht (v*)	→ aussehen
das Buch –(e)s,¨-er (nn)	book
einfach (adv)	simply, quite
erster/erste/erstes (adj)	first
erzählen (v)	to tell
flippe aus (v*)	→ ausflippen
die Fortsetzung -, -en (nf)	next instalment, continuation
die Frau -,-en (nf)	woman
der Freund -(e)s,-e (nm)	boyfriend
gelesen (v*)	→ lesen
genau (adv)	exactly
gleich (adv)	the same
gut (adv)	well
haargenau (adv)	exactly
hässlich (adj)	ugly
heißen (v*)	to be called
heißt (v*)	→ heißen
ja schließlich	after all
ja wirklich	really
jung (adj)	young
der Klappentext –es,-e (nm)	blurb
klasse (adj)	great
das Leben –s,- (nn)	life
lesen (v*)	to read
die Literatur -,-en (nf)	literature
mal = einmal	once
der Mist –(e)s (nm)	rubbish
na gut	well all right
nach Abzug der Steuern	after tax
der Name –ns,-n (nm)	name
natürlich (adv)	of course, naturally
romantisch (adj)	romantic
schlecht (adj)	bad
sich interessieren (v)	to be interested
sich verkaufen (v)	to sell
sieh mal	look
das Spiegelbild –(e)s,-er (nn)	reflection
die Toilette -,-n (nf)	toilet
ungewöhnlich (adj)	unusual
unglaublich (adj)	incredible
unlesbar (adj)	unreadable
weil (conj)	because
wenn (conj)	if
wo (adv)	where
zahlen (v)	to pay

Numbers

zero	null
one	eins
two	zwei
three	drei
four	vier
five	fünf
six	sechs
seven	sieben
eight	acht
nine	neun
ten	zehn
eleven	elf
twelve	zwölf
thirteen	dreizehn
fourteen	vierzehn
fifteen	fünfzehn
sixteen	sechzehn
seventeen	siebzehn
eighteen	achtzehn
nineteen	neunzehn
twenty	zwanzig
twenty-one	einundzwanzig
twenty-two	zweiundzwanzig
twenty-three	dreiundzwanzig
twenty-four	vierundzwanzig
twenty-five	fünfundzwanzig
twenty-six	sechsundzwanzig
twenty-seven	siebenundzwanzig
twenty-eight	achtundzwanzig
twenty-nine	neunundzwanzig
thirty	dreißig
forty	vierzig
fifty	fünfzig
sixty	sechzig
seventy	siebzig
eighty	achtzig
ninety	neunzig
hundred	hundert
thousand	tausend
a million	eine Million

When speaking to a person or a group of people you do not know very well, the polite form Sie/ Ihr/Ihnen (you, your) is used.

Key Structures

Kein Wunder	it's not surprising, no wonder
Wie war der Name noch?	What was the name again?
wie ist Ihr Name?	what is your name?
Als ich ... gelesen habe, wäre ich beinah in Ohnmacht gefallen	I nearly fainted when I read ....
Schlagen Sie Gewinn heraus?	Do you make a profit?
dass mein Freund anders heißt	that my friend is called something else, that my friend has a different name
was würden Sie zahlen?	how much would you pay?

WIEDERGEBURT

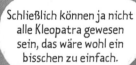

Religion and Beliefs

Understanding the text

aha (interj)	oh, I see
anders (adj)	different
bin (v*)	→ sein
China –s (nn)	China
dann (adv)	then
darf (v*)	→ dürfen
darf ich	may I
darüber (adv)	about it
das (pron)	that
du selbst (pron)	you yourself
dürfen (v*)	to be allowed
ein bisschen zu einfach	a bit too simple
erbärmlich (adj)	pathetic
erinnern (v)	to remind
erst (adv)	first
euer (adj)	your
früher (adj)	previous
ganz (adv)	very, pretty, quite
ganz schön	pretty
grausam (adj)	cruel
haben (v*)	to have
hart (adj)	hard
heißen (v*)	to be called
die Inkaprinzessin –,-nen (nf)	Inca princess
das Jahrhundert –s,-e (nn)	century
klar (interj)	sure
Kleopatra – (nf)	Cleopatra
die Königin –,-nen (nf)	queen
lauter (adj)	nothing but
das Leben –s,- (nn)	life
machen (v)	to do
mächtig (adj)	powerful

natürlich (adv)	of course
niemand (pron)	nobody
der Prinz –en,-en (nm)	prince
das Recht –(e)s,-e (nn)	right
schließlich (adv)	after all
sein (v*)	to be
sich aussprechen (v sep*)	to talk
der Sultan –s,-e (nm)	sultan
das Volk –(e)s,¨-er (nn)	people
war, warst, wart (v*)	→ sein
weil (conj)	because
die Wiedergeburt –,-en (nf)	reincarnation
wirklich (adv)	really

⮑ Key Structures

und dann blieb niemand übrig, der zum Volk gehörte	and then there was nobody left who belonged to the people
was weißt du denn überhaupt?	what do you know about it?
weil du wohl selbst Kleopatra warst, oder?	because you were Cleopatra yourself, were you? because you were Cleopatra yourself, I suppose?

oder is used in a question: question tags such as **oder?, nicht wahr?, ja?** correspond to isn't it?, aren't you?, or is it?, etc.

Darf ich dich daran erinnern	May I remind you

daran (of it) does not need to be translated

sie stammen aus dem 14. Jahrhundert	they date back to the 14th century.

ordinal numbers are usually written as figures followed by a full stop.

im 22. Jahrhundert	in the 22nd century

⮑ Religion and Beliefs

Buddhism	der Buddhismus
Buddhist (n)	der Buddhist/die Buddhistin
Buddhist (adj)	buddhistisch
Christianity	das Christentum
Christian (n)	der Christ/die Christin
Christian (adj)	christlich
Jewish	jüdisch
Islam	der Islam
Muslim (n)	der Moslem/die Moslime
Muslim (adj)	moslemisch
atheist	der Atheist/die Atheistin
believer	der Gläubige/die Gläubige
the Bible	die Bibel
the Koran	der Koran
Catholic	katholisch
Orthodox	orthodox
Protestant	protestantisch
to believe in God	an Gott glauben
he is an atheist	er ist ein Atheist
pope	der Papst
priest	der Priester
sermon	die Predigt
church	die Kirche
mosque	die Moschee

GLOSSARY

A

abends	(adv)	in the evening	41
aber	(conj)	but	
Abflughalle -,-n	(nf)	departure lounge	59
abhauen ©	(v sep)	to beat it, to leave	13
abholen	(v sep)	to collect, pick up	59
Abitur -s	(nn)	A-levels	15
abmachen	(v sep)	to take off	31
abnehmen	(v sep*)	to lose weight	57
abrufen	(v sep*)	to call up	39
abschleppen ©	(v sep)	to get off with	33
abschreiben	(v sep*)	to crib, to copy	47
absetzen	(v sep)	to drop off	59
Abstecher -s,-	(nm)	side-trip	29
Abteil -(e)s,-e	(nn)	compartment	59
abwerten	(v sep)	to devalue	55
ach	(int)	oh	25, 27, 43, 53
acht	(number)	eight	29, 65
achtundzwanzig	(number)	twenty-eight	65
achtzehn	(number)	eighteen	65
achtzig	(number)	eighty	65
Aerobic -s	(nn)	aerobics	9, 21, 61
Afrikaner -s,-/Afrikanerin -,-nen	(nm/f)	African	35
ah	(interj)	oh, ah	53
aha	(interj)	oh, I see	67
Aktie -,-n	(nf)	share	63
Aktionär -s,-e/Aktionärin -,-nen	(nm/f)	shareholder	63
Album -s, Alben	(nn)	album	21
alle	(pron pl)	all, everybody	
allein	(adv)	alone	15
aller/alle/alles	(pron)	all	
allergisch	(adj)	allergic	49
alles	(pron)	everything	
als	(conj)	when	61, 65
also	(adv)	well;	11, 19, 37, 53, 55;
		well, all right then;	25;
		so	43
alt	(adj)	old	9, 29, 53
am	(prep)	on	37
am = an dem	(prep)	at	59
amerikanisch	(adj)	American	29, 37
amüsieren, sich	(v)	to have fun	33
anderer/andere/anderes	(adj)	other	9, 51
anders	(adj)	different	67
Änderung -,-en	(nf)	alteration	11
anfangen	(v sep*)	to do	31, 57
angeblich	(adv)	apparently, they say that ...	37
Angebot -(e)s,-e	(nn)	supply	63
angehen	(v sep*)	to tackle	35
angerufen	(v*)	→ anrufen	41
Angestellte -n,-n	(nm/f)	employee	55
Angst -, Ängste	(nf)	fear	15, 41
anhaben	(v sep*)	to wear, to have on	51, 61
anklicken	(v sep)	to click on	39
Anlage -,-n	(nf)	attachment	39
anmachen ©	(v sep)	to chat up	33
Anruf -(e)s,-e	(nm)	call	11
Anrufbeantworter -s,-	(nm)	answering machine	35
anrufen	(v sep*)	to ring, to phone, to call	
ansteckend	(adj)	infectious	49
Anteil -(e)s,-e	(nm)	share	63
Antenne -,-n	(nf)	aerial	53
antworten	(v)	to answer, to reply	61, 63
Anweisung -,-en	(nf)	instruction	35
anziehen	(v sep*)	to dress	51
anziehen, sich	(v sep*)	to get dressed	51
Apfel -s/¨-	(nm)	apple	43
Apfelkuchen -s,-	(nm)	apple-cake	43

Apparat -(e)s,-e	(nn)	extension number	35
Appartement -s,-s	(nn)	flat, apartment	19
April	(nm)	April	27
Äquator -s	(nm)	equator	47
Arbeit -,-en	(nf)	paper	47
arbeiten	(v)	to work	15, 23
Arbeiter -s,-/Arbeiterin -,-nen	(nm/f)	worker	55
Arbeitslosengeld -(e)s,-er	(nn)	unemployment benefit	63
Arbeitslosigkeit -,-en	(nf)	unemployment	63
Arbeitszeit -,-en	(nf)	working hours	55
Architektur -	(nf)	architecture	45
Ärger -s	(nm)	anger	41
arm	(adj)	poor	53
Arm -(e)s,-e	(nm)	arm	57
Asthma -s	(nn)	asthma	49
Atheist -en,-en/Atheistin -,-nen	(nm/f)	atheist	67
ätzend ©	(adj)	disgusting, awful	19, 31
auch	(adv)	also, too	
auf	(prep)	on	23, 51
aufführen	(v sep)	to perform	45
Aufführung -,-en	(nf)	performance (of a play)	45
aufgeben	(v sep*)	to give up	55
aufkleben	(v sep)	to stick on	23
auflegen	(v sep)	to hang up	35
aufnehmen	(v sep*)	to record	45
aufräumen	(v sep)	to tidy up	13, 49
Aufschnitt -(e)s	(nm)	cold meats	43
aufstehen	(v sep*)	to get up	63
Auge -s,-n	(nn)	eye	57
Augenbraue -,-n	(nf)	eyebrow	57
Augenlid -(e)s,-er	(nn)	eyelid	57
Augenwimper -,-n	(nf)	eyelash	57
August	(nm)	August	27
Ausbildung -,-en	(nf)	education	55
Ausbildungsplatz -(e)s,¨-e	(nm)	training place	15
ausdrucken	(v sep)	to print	39
ausflippen ©	(v sep)	to go mad	65
ausgehen	(v sep*)	to go out	13
ausmachen	(v sep)	to arrange	35
ausquatschen ©	(v sep)	to let out	33
aussehen	(v sep*)	to look;	51, 65;
		to look like	29
Außenhandel -s	(nm)	foreign trade	63
außer	(prep)	except (for)	9, 13
außerdem	(adv)	besides;	27;
		in addition, as well as	29
aussieht	(v*)	→ aussehen	29, 65
aussprechen, sich	(v sep*)	to talk	67
Ausstellung -,-en	(nf)	exhibition	45
Ausweis -es,-e	(nm)	identity card	13
Auto -s,-s	(nn)	car	35, 59
Autor -s,-en/ Autorin -,-nen	(nm/f)	author;	45;
		writer	55
Autowerkstatt -,¨-en	(nf)	garage	11
auweia	(interj)	oh dear	41

B

B-Sprache -,-n	(nf)	secret language	63
Baby -s,-s	(nn)	baby	17
babysitten	(v)	to babysit	43
Babysitter -s,-	(nm)	babysitter	43
Babysitting -s	(nn)	baby-sitting	61
Backe -,-n	(nf)	cheek	57
Badeanzug -(e)s,¨-e	(nm)	swimming costume	51
Badehose -,-n	(nf)	trunks	51
Badezimmer -s,-	(nn)	bathroom	9, 19
Badminton -	(nn)	badminton	61
Bahnhof -(e)s,¨-e	(nm)	(railway) station	29, 59
Balg -(e)s,¨-er ©	(nn)	brat	43

Ballett -(e)s,-e	(nn)	ballet	13, 45	
Banane -,-n	(nf)	banana	43	
Band -,-s	(nf)	band	53	
Bank -,-en	(nf)	bank	31	
Bankangestellte -n,-n	(nm/f)	bank clerk	55	
Bankkonto -s,-s	(nn)	bank account	31	
Barbecue -(s),-s	(nn)	barbecue	59	
Bargeld -(e)s	(nn)	cash	31	
Bart -(e)s,"-e	(nm)	beard	9	
Batterie -,-n	(nf)	battery	49	
Bauch -(e)s,"-e	(nm)	stomach, tummy	57	
Bausparkasse -,-n	(nf)	building society	31	
beantworten	(v)	to answer	11, 47	
bedeuten	(v)	to mean	49	
Beerdigung -,-en	(nf)	funeral	27	
bei	(prep)	at	13, 41	
beide	(adj)	both	23	
Bein -(e)s,-e	(nn)	leg	57	
Beispiel -(e)s,-e	(nn)	example	49, 55	
Bekannte -n,-n	(nm/f)	acquaintance	33	
bekommen	(v*)	to receive	39	
belegt	(adj)	full	29	
benutzen	(v)	to use	39	
Berg -(e)s,-e	(nm)	mountain	47	
Beruf -(e)s,-e	(nm)	profession	55	
Berufsleben -s	(nn)	professional life	57	
Beruhigungspille -,-n	(nf)	tranquilliser, sedative (pill)	49	
bescheuert	(adj)	stupid	33	
besetzt	(adj)	engaged	23, 35	
besorgt	(adj)	worried, concerned	41	
bestehen	(v*)	to pass	15	
bestimmt	(adv)	certainly, definitely	33, 45, 59	
Besuch -(e)s,-e	(nm)	visit	27	
Betrag -(e)s,"-e	(nm)	sum, amount	39	
bezahlen	(v)	to pay (for)	61	
Bibel -,-n	(nf)	Bible	67	
Bier -(e)s,-e	(nn)	beer	43	
Bildhauerei -,-en	(nf)	sculpture	45	
Bildschirm -(e)s,-e	(nm)	screen	39	
bin	(v*)	→ sein		
Birne -,-n	(nf)	bulb; pear	25; 43	
bist	(v*)	→ sein		
bitte	(adv)	please		
bleiben	(v*)	to stay	21	
Blitz -(e)s,-e	(nm)	lightning	47	
Blumenkohl -(e)s	(nm)	cauliflower	43	
Bluse -,-n	(nf)	blouse	51	
Blut -(e)s	(nn)	blood	55	
Börse -,-n	(nf)	stock exchange	63	
böse	(adj)	angry	41	
Bote -n,-n	(nm)	courier	23	
Boxershort -,-s	(nf)	boxer shorts	51	
Branchenverzeichnis -ses,-se	(nn)	Yellow Pages	35	
Brathähnchen -s,-	(nn)	roast chicken	43	
Breitbild-Fernseher -s,-	(nm)	widescreen TV	43	
Brief -(e)s,-e	(nm)	letter	23	
Briefträger -s,-	(nm)	postman	23	
Briefumschlag -(e)s,"-e	(nm)	envelope	23	
Brille -,-n	(nf)	glasses	9	
Brot -(e)s	(nn)	bread	43	
Bruder -s,"-	(nm)	brother	11, 17, 27	
Brust -	(nf)	chest	57	
Bruttoeinkommen -s	(nn)	gross income	63	
Buch -(e)s,"-er	(nn)	book	53, 65	
Buchhalter -s,-/Buchhalterin -,-nen	(nm/f)	accountant	55	
Buddhismus -	(nm)	Buddhism	67	
Buddhist -en,-en/Buddhistin -,-nen	(nm/f)	Buddhist	67	
buddhistisch	(adj)	Buddhist	67	
büffeln	(v)	to revise	13	
Bulle -n,-n	(nm)	cop	13	
Büro -s,-s	(nn)	office, study	63	
Bürohaus -es,"-er	(nn)	office block	19	
Bus -ses,-se	(nm)	bus	39, 59	
Busbahnhof -(e)s,"-e	(nm)	coach station	29	
Busen -s,-	(nm)	breasts, bosom	57	
Bushaltestelle -,-n	(nf)	bus stop	59	
Büstenhalter -s,-	(nm)	bra	51	
Butter -	(nf)	butter	43	

C

Café -s,-s	(nn)	café	59	
CD -,-(s)	(nf)	CD	21, 25	
Chef -s,-s/ Chefin -,-nen	(nm/f)	boss	55	
chemische Reinigung	(nf)	dry cleaner's	11	
China -s	(nn)	China	67	
Chips	(nm pl)	crisps	43	
Chirurg -s,-en/Chirurgin -,-nen	(nm/f)	surgeon	55	
Christ -en,-en/ Christin -,-nen	(nm/f)	Christian	67	
Christentum -s	(nn)	Christianity	67	
christlich	(adj)	Christian	67	
clever	(adj)	clever	29	
Cola -(s),-s	(nn)	coke	43	
Comicheft -(e)s,-e	(nn)	comic	9	
Comicstrip -s,-s	(nm)	comic strip	45	
Computer -s,-	(nm)	computer	39	
Computerausdruck -(e)s,-e	(nm)	computer print-out	23	
Computerspiel -(e)s,-e	(nn)	computer game	21	
cool	(adj)	brilliant; great, cool	29; 33	
Cursor -s,-s	(nm)	cursor	39	

D

da	(adv)	here, there		
dabei	(adv)	during this; although; and yet	13; 47; 19	
Daddy -s,-s	(nm)	daddy, father	29	
Dame -,-n	(nf)	lady	29, 61	
damit	(conj)	so that	11	
danach	(adv)	afterwards	13, 57	
danke (schön)	(adv)	thanks, thank you		
dann	(adv)	then		
darf	(v*)	→ dürfen	67	
Darlehen -s,-	(nn)	loan	15	
darüber	(adv)	about it	67	
darum	(adv)	that's why	49	
das	(pron)	that, it		
dass	(conj)	that		
Datei -,-en	(nf)	file	39	
dein	(pron)	your		
denen	(pron)	(to) whom		
denken	(v*)	to think	13, 31	
deprimiert	(adj)	depressed	41	
der	(pron)	he; which	13; 45	
der/die/das	(art)	the		
Deutschland -s	(nn)	Germany	35	
Dezember	(nm)	December	27	
dich	(pron)	you		
Dichtung -	(nf)	poetry	45	
dick	(adj)	big	53	
die	(pron)	who, which	9	
Diele -,-n	(nf)	hall	39	
Dienstag	(nm)	Tuesday	27	
Dienstleistungsbetrieb -(e)s,-e	(nm)	service industry	63	
dieser/diese/dieses	(adj)	this, (pl) these		

GLOSSARY continued

Digitalfernsehen -s	(nn)	digital TV	53
Ding -(e)s,-e	(nn)	thing	39
dir	(pron)	(to) you	
Diskette -,-n	(nf)	(floppy) disk	39
Disko-,-s	(nf)	disco	13
Dokumentarfilm -(e)s,-e	(nm)	documentary film	13, 53
Donner -s	(nm)	thunder	47
Donnerstag	(nm)	Thursday	27
Doppelzimmer -s,-	(nn)	double room	19, 29
Dorf -(e)s,¨-er	(nn)	village	59
drei	(number)	three	29, 57, 61, 65
Dreibettzimmer -s,-	(nn)	a room with three beds	29
dreißig	(number)	thirty	65
dreiundzwanzig	(number)	twenty-three	65
dreizehn	(number)	thirteen	65
Drucker -s,-	(nm)	printer	39
du	(pron)	you	
dünn	(adj)	thin	9
Durchfall -s	(nm)	diarrhoea	49
durchfallen	(v sep*)	to fail an exam	47
durchgehend	(adj)	through	59
durchkommen	(v sep*)	to get through	23
Durchschnittsnote -,-n	(nf)	average mark	47
dürfen	(v*)	to be allowed	67

E

E-Mail -,-s	(nf)	e-mail	23, 39
E-Mail-Adresse -,-n	(nf)	e-mail address	39
eben	(adv)	just	51
ehrgeizig	(adj)	ambitious	9
ehrlich	(adv)	honestly	33
Eifersucht	(nf)	jealousy	41
eifersüchtig	(adj)	jealous	41
eigentlich	(adv)	actually	27, 63
ein/eine/ein	(art)	a, an	17
Einbauküche -,-n	(nf)	fitted kitchen	19
einfach	(adj);	easy, simple;	23;
	(adv)	simply	19, 45, 65
einführen	(v sep)	to insert	
eingeben	(v sep*)	to enter, key in	39
eingeschlossen	(v*)	→ einschließen	9
Einkommenssteuer -	(nf)	income tax	63
einladen	(v sep*)	to invite	27, 29
einlegen	(v sep)	to put in, to insert	49
einlösen	(v sep)	to cash	31
einmal	(adv)	once;	27, 35;
		one day, some day	49
einplanen	(v sep)	to plan, to allow for	57
eins	(number)	one	65
Eins -,-en	(nf)	one	47
einsam	(adv)	lonely	9
einschließen	(v sep*)	to lock in	9
einundzwanzig	(number)	twenty-one	65
einwerfen	(v sep*)	to post, mail;	23;
		to insert	31
Einzelhandelspreis -es,-e	(nm)	retail price	63
Einzelzimmer -s,-	(nn)	single room	19, 29
Einzimmerwohnung -,-en	(nf)	one-bedroom flat	19
Eis -es	(nn)	ice	47
elf	(number)	eleven	65
Ellbogen -s,-	(nm)	elbow	57
Eltern	(npl)	parents	13, 17, 37
endlich	(adv)	at last, finally	13, 29
Endnote -,-n	(nf)	final mark	47
entscheidend	(adj)	decisive	49
Entscheidung -,-en	(nf)	decision	33
entwachsen	(v*)	to outgrow,	
		to grow out of	29
Entwicklung -,-en	(nf)	development	47

er	(pron)	he	
erbärmlich	(adj)	pathetic	67
Erbse -,-n	(nf)	pea	43
Erdbeere -,-n	(nf)	strawberry	43
Erde -	(nf)	earth	47
Erdnuss -,¨-e	(nf)	peanut	43
Erdteil -(e)s,-e	(nm)	continent	47
erfolgreich	(adj)	successful	57
erhalten	(v*)	to receive	39
erinnern	(v)	to remind	67
erlauben	(v)	to allow	41
Ersatzteil -(e)s,-e	(nn)	spare part	11
Erschließung -,-en	(nf)	development, tapping	47
Ersparnisse	(npl)	savings	31
erst	(adv)	first	67
Erste -n,-n	(nm/f)	first (one)	13
erstens	(adv)	firstly	33
erster/erste/erstes	(adj)	first	
Erwachsenenbildung -	(nf)	adult education	15
erwarten	(v)	to expect,	
		to be waiting for	11
erwischen	(v)	to catch	13
erzählen	(v)	to tell	19, 65
erziehen	(v)	to bring up	17
es	(pron)	it	
Essen -s,-	(nn)	meal	27
Essig -s	(nm)	vinegar	43
Esszimmer -s,-	(nn)	dining room	19
etwa	(adv)	perhaps	11
etwas	(pron)	something	45
euch	(pron)	you	59
euer	(adj)	your	67
Euroscheck -s,-s	(nm)	Eurocheque	31
Export -(e)s,-e	(nm)	export	63

F

fahre hin	(v*)	→ hinfahren	59
fahre runter	(v*)	→ runterfahren	61
fahren	(v*)	to go	37
Fahrer -s,-/ Fahrerin -,-nen	(nm/f)	driver	55
Fahrrad -(e)s,¨-er	(nn)	bicycle	59
Fahrstuhl -(e)s,¨-e	(nm)	lift	61
fallen	(v*)	to go down	19
falsch	(adj)	wrong	11
Familie -,-n	(nf)	family	37
Familienleben -s	(nn)	family life	57
famos	(adj)	splendid	25
faszinieren	(v)	to fascinate	39
faul	(adj)	lazy	9
Fax -,-(e)	(nn)	fax	23
Faxgerät -(e)s,-e	(nn)	fax machine	23
Faxnummer -,-n	(nf)	fax number	23
Februar	(nm)	February	27
Federball -(e)s	(nm)	badminton	21, 61
Fehlentscheidung -,-en	(nf)	wrong decision	47
Fehlkalkulation -,-en	(nf)	miscalculation, mistake	55
Feiertag, gesetzlicher	(nm)	bank/national holiday/	
		vacation	37
Feingefühl -(e)s	(nn)	sensitivity	33
Ferien	(npl)	holidays, vacation	37
Fernbedienung -	(nf)	remote control	53
Fernmeldewesen -s	(nn)	telecommunications	53
fernsehen	(v sep*)	to watch TV	21, 53
Fernsehen -s	(nn)	television	21, 23, 53
Fernseher -s,-	(nm)	television (set)	53
Fernsehserie -,-n	(nf)	TV series	53
Fest -(e)s,-e	(nn)	party	13
Festival -s,-s	(nn)	festival	13
festnehmen	(v sep*)	to take in, to arrest	13

Festplatte -,-n	(nf)	hard disk	39
feststehen	(v sep*)	to be certain	55
Fete -,-n ⓔ	(nf)	party	25
fett	(adj)	fat	9
Feuerwehrmann -(e)s,¨-er	(nm)	fire officer	55
Film -(e)s,-e	(nm)	film	13
filmen	(v)	to film	45
finden	(v*)	to find	19, 25, 41
Finger -s,-	(nm)	finger	57
Firma -,-men	(nf)	firm	63
Fisch -es,-e	(nm)	fish	43
fit	(adj)	fit	57
Fitness -	(nf)	fitness	61
Fitnesscenter -s,-	(nn)	gym	57
Fitnesstraining -s	(nn)	fitness training, keeping fit	61
fliegen	(v*)	to fly	59
flippe aus	(v*)	→ ausflippen	65
Flohmarkt -(e)s,¨-e	(nm)	flea market	37
Fluggesellschaft -,-en	(nf)	airline	11
Flughafen -s,¨-	(nm)	airport	29, 59
Flugzeug -(e)s,-e	(nn)	plane	59
Fluss -es,¨-e	(nm)	river	47
Fortsetzung -, -en	(nf)	next instalment, continuation	65
Foto -s,-s	(nn)	photo	51
Frage -,-n	(nf)	question	9, 33, 47
fragen	(v)	to ask	43, 59, 63
fragt	(v)	→ fragen	43
Frau -,-en	(nf)	wife; woman	23; 61, 65
freiberuflich	(adj)	freelance	55
Freitag	(nm)	Friday	27
Freizeichen -s,-	(nn)	dialling tone	35
Freizeit -	(nf)	leisure	21
Fremdenverkehr -s	(nm)	tourism	63
Freude -,-n	(nf)	pleasure	41
freuen, sich	(v)	to be pleased	31
Freund -(e)s,-e	(nm)	friend; boyfriend	33, 39; 13, 33, 59, 65
Freundin -,-nen	(nf)	(girl)friend	33, 43
Freundschaft -	(nf)	friendship	33
Friseur -s,-e/ Friseuse -,-n	(nm/f)	hairdresser	55
Frost -(e)s	(nm)	frost	47
Fruchtsaft -(e)s,¨-e	(nm)	fruit juice	43
früherer/frühere/früheres	(adj)	earlier, previous	49, 67
Frühstück -(e)s,-e	(nn)	breakfast	29
Frühzeit -,-en	(nf)	early period, early life	65
fühlen, sich	(v)	to feel	15
füllen	(v)	to fill	13
fünf	(number)	five	65
fünfundzwanzig	(number)	twenty-five	65
fünfzehn	(number)	fifteen	65
fünfzig	(number)	fifty	65
für	(prep)	for	
furchtbar	(adj)	horrible; terrible; awful;	15; 51, 55; 53;
	(adv)	terribly	27, 31, 33
Fuß -es,¨-e	(nm)	foot	57
Fußball -(e)s	(nm)	football/soccer	21, 61
Fußtritt -(e)s,-e	(nm)	kick	25

G

Gameshow -,-s	(nf)	game show	53
ganz	(adj);	whole;	13;
	(adv)	completely; very, really	43; 53, 67
Ganztagsstelle -,-n	(nf)	full-time job	55

Garage -,-n	(nf)	garage	19
Garten -s,¨-	(nm)	garden	19, 53
Gast -(e)s,¨-e	(nm)	guest	37
geben	(v*)	to give	47, 53
Gebrauchtwagen -s,-	(nm)	second-hand car	11
Geburtstag -(e)s,-e	(nm)	birthday	27, 45
Geburtstagsgeschenk -(e)s,-e	(nn)	birthday present	45
Geburtstagskarte -,-n	(nf)	birthday card	45
Gefühlsleben -s	(nn)	emotional life	57
gefunden	(v*)	→ finden	19
gegangen	(v*)	→ gehen	27
Gegensprechanlage -,-n	(nf)	intercom	23
gegenwärtig	(adj)	present	49
gegossen	(v*)	→ gießen	13
Gehalt -(e)s,¨-er	(nn)	salary	55
Gehaltserhöhung -,-en	(nf)	pay rise	31
Geheimnummer -,-n	(nf)	PIN (number)	31
Geheimseite -,-n	(nf)	secret page	39
gehen	(v*)	to go; to walk, to go	21, 27, 43, 63 61
Gehirn -(e)s,-e	(nn)	brain	57
gehst	(v*)	→ gehen	43
geil	(interj)	cool, brilliant	31
Geistesblitz -es,-e	(nm)	brainwave, flash of inspiration	37
gekommen	(v*)	→ kommen	13
geküsst	(v)	→ küssen	33
Geld -(e)s,-er	(nn)	money	21, 31, 39
Geldautomat -en,-en	(nm)	cashpoint, cash machine	31
Geldschein -(e)s,-e	(nm)	banknote	31
gelesen	(v*)	→ lesen	65
Gemälde -s,-	(nn)	painting	45
genau	(adj);	precise, exact	35;
	(adv)	exactly	51, 65
genauso	(adv)	just the same	63
Gequassel -s	(nn)	jabbering	27
gerade	(adv)	just	13, 35
gerufen	(v*)	→ rufen	13
Gesamtschule -,-n	(nf)	comprehensive school	15
Geschäfte	(npl)	business	63
Geschäftsanteil -(e)s,-e	(nm)	share	63
Geschäftsfrau -,-en	(nf)	businesswoman	55
Geschäftsjahr -(e)s,-e	(nn)	financial year	63
Geschäftsmann -(e)s,¨-er	(nm)	businessman	55
geschält	(adj)	peeled	35
Geschenk -(e)s,-e	(nn)	present	31
geschenkt	(v)	→ schenken	31
Geschichte -,-n	(nf)	story	45
Geschichtsstunde -,-n	(nf)	history class	15
geschieden	(adj)	divorced	17
Geschirrspüler -s,-	(nm)	dishwasher	19
geschlafen	(v*)	→ schlafen	41
geschmissen	(v*)	→ schmeißen	13
geschrieben	(v*)	→ schreiben	47
gesehen	(v*)	→ sehen	19
Gesellschaft -,-en	(nf)	company	63
gestern	(adv)	yesterday	61
gesund	(adj)	well	49
getroffen	(v*)	→ treffen	25
gewesen	(v*)	→ sein	65
gib	(v*)	→ geben	9, 53
gießen	(v*)	to pour	13
Gitarre -,-n	(nf)	guitar	9
glatt	(adj)	straight	9
glauben	(v)	to think; to believe	59, 63; 63, 67
Gläubige -n,-n	(nm/f)	believer	67
gleich	(adj);	same;	51;
	(adv)	the same; immediately	65; 13, 61

GLOSSARY continued

Gleis -es,-e	(nn)	platform	59
Glück -(e)s	(nn)	happiness	41
Golf -s	(nn)	golf	21
Gott -(e)s,¨-er	(nm)	god	67
Grafik -	(nf)	graphic art	45
grausam	(adj)	cruel	67
griechisch	(adj)	Greek	53
Grippe	(nf)	flu	49
groß	(adj)	tall;	9;
		big, large	33, 45
Großhandelspreis -es,-e	(nm)	wholesale price	63
Großmutter -,¨-	(nf)	grandmother	17, 35
Großonkel -s,-	(nm)	great uncle	27
Großvater -s,¨-	(nm)	grandfather	17
grün	(adj)	green	57
Grundschule -,-n	(nf)	primary school	15
Gurke -,-n	(nf)	cucumber	43
Gürtel -s,-	(nm)	belt	51
gut	(adj);	all right, OK;	25
		good;	55;
	(adv)	well	65;
gut aussehend	(adj)	good-looking	9
Gymnasium -s,-ien	(nn)	grammar school	15

H

Haar -(e)s,-e	(nn)	hair	57
haargenau	(adv)	exactly	65
habe an	(v*)	→ anhaben	61
haben	(v*)	to have	
hacken	(v)	to hack	39
Hacker -s,-	(nm)	hacker	39
Hafen -s,¨-	(nm)	port;	29;
		harbour	59
Halbkugel -,-n	(nf)	hemisphere	47
Halbpension -	(nf)	half board	29
Hälfte -,-n	(nf)	half	33
hallo	(interj)	hi, hello	21, 35, 43, 53
Halogenlampe -,-n	(nf)	halogen lamp	13
Hals -es,¨-e	(nm)	neck	57
halt	(interj)	stop	39
Hand -,¨-e	(nf)	hand	33, 57
Handelsbilanz -	(nf)	balance of trade	63
Handgelenk -(e)s,-e	(nn)	wrist	57
Handschuh -(e)s,-e	(nm)	glove	51
Handy -s,-s	(nn)	mobile (phone)	23
hart	(adj)	hard	67
hassen	(v)	to hate	21
hässlich	(adj)	ugly	9, 65
hast	(v*)	→ haben	
hat	(v*)	→ haben	
hatte	(v*)	→ haben	
Hauptperson -,-en	(nf)	most important person, star	45
Hauptschule -,-n	(nf)	secondary school	15
Hausaufgaben	(npl)	homework	21
Hausmeister -s,-/ Hausmeisterin -,-nen	(nm/f)	caretaker	55
Haustür -,-en	(nf)	front door	23
he	(interj)	hey	11
heiraten	(v)	to get married;	17;
		to marry	55
heiß	(adj)	hot;	21;
		brilliant	43
heißen	(v*)	to be called	27, 65, 67
heißt	(v*)	→ heißen	65
Hemd -(e)s,-en	(nn)	shirt	51
Hemisphäre -,-n	(nf)	hemisphere	47
herrlich	(adj)	magnificent	49
herumreisen	(v sep)	to travel around, about	15
Herz -ens,-en	(nn)	heart	57

Heuschnupfen -s	(nm)	hayfever	49
heute	(adv)	today	35
heutzutage	(adv)	nowadays	23
hier	(adv)	here	9, 11
hierher	(adv)	here	39
Highlight -(s),-s	(nn)	highlight	29
Himbeere -,-n	(nf)	raspberry	43
Himmel -s	(nm)	sky	47
hinfahren	(v sep*)	to drive there	59
hingehen	(v sep*)	to go (there)	23
hinsetzen, sich	(v sep)	to sit down	63
Hintern -s,- ⊚	(nm)	behind, bottom	25, 57
Hitparade -,-n	(nf)	hit parade, Top of the Pops	53
hochgehen	(v sep*)	to walk up, go up	61
Hockey -s	(nn)	hockey	61
Hoffnung -,-en	(nf)	hope	15
höflich	(adj)	polite	9
hole ab	(v)	→ abholen	59
holen	(v)	to fetch, to get	61
homöopathisch	(adj)	homeopathic	55
hören	(v)	to listen to	21
Hörer -s,-	(nm)	receiver	35
hörst zu	(v)	→ zuhören	29
hört mit	(v)	→ mithören	63
Hose -,-n	(nf)	(pair of) trousers	51
Hotel -s,-s	(nn)	hotel	29
hübsch	(adj)	pretty	55
Hüfte -,-n	(nf)	hip	57
Huhn -(e)s,¨-er	(nn)	chicken	43
hundert	(number)	hundred	65
Hypothek -,-en	(nf)	mortgage	63

I

IC	(nm)	intercity train	59
ich	(pron)	I, me	
Ich -(s),-(s)	(nn)	self	9
ihn	(pron)	him, it	
Ihnen	(pron)	(to) you	
ihr	(pron)	her, your	
Ihr	(adj)	your	
Illusion -.-en	(nf)	illusion	15
im = in dem	(prep)	in	39, 63
immer	(adv)	always	
Import -(e)s,-e	(nm)	import	63
in	(prep)	in, into	
Industrie -,-n	(nf)	industry	63
Ingenieur -s,-e/ Ingenieurin -,-nen	(nm/f)	engineer	55
Inkaprinzessin -,-nen	(nf)	Inca princess	67
Inliner	(nm pl)	rollerblades, inline skates	33, 61
innerhalb	(prep)	within	45
ins = in das	(prep)	into	
Installateur -s,-e	(nm)	plumber	55
intelligent	(adj)	intelligent	9
Intercityzug -(e)s,¨-e	(nm)	intercity train	59
interessant	(adj)	interesting	39
interessieren, sich	(v)	to be interested	65
Internet -s,-s	(nn)	Internet	21, 39, 43
inzwischen	(adv)	by now	55
irgendein	(pron)	any	21
irgendjemand	(pron)	somebody	13
irgendwas = irgendetwas	(pron)	something	63
irgendwo	(adv)	somewhere, anywhere	9
irre ⊚	(adv)	terribly	61
Islam -s	(nm)	Islam	67
ist	(v*)	→ sein	

J

ja	(adv)	yes	
Jacke -,-n	(nf)	jacket	51
Jahr -(e)s,-e	(nn)	year	19, 29
Jahresumsatz -es	(nm)	annual turnover	63
Jahrhundert -s,-e	(nn)	century	67
Jahrmarkt -(e)s,¨-e	(nm)	funfair	13
Januar	(nm)	January	27
Jazzmusik -	(nf)	jazz, jazz music	29
Jeans	(nf or pl)	jeans	51
jedenfalls	(adv)	in any case, anyway	51
jeder/jede/jedes	(adj)	every	29
jemand	(pron)	somebody, someone	13, 63
jetzt	(adv)	now	
joggen	(v)	to jog	61
Joggingschuh -(e)s,-e	(nm)	jogging/running shoe	61
Joghurt -(s),-(s)	(nm)	yoghurt	43
Journalist -en,-en/ Journalistin -,-nen	(nm/f)	journalist	55
jüdisch	(adj)	Jewish	67
Jugend -	(nf)	youth	15
Jugendherberge -,-n	(nf)	youth hostel	29
Juli -(s),-s	(nm)	July	27, 29
jung	(adj)	young	15, 29, 33, 65
Junge -n,-n	(nm)	boy, lad	29, 41
Juni -	(nm)	June	27
Jura	(npl)	law	15
jurassisch	(adj)	Jurassic	65

K

Kaffee -s,-s	(nm)	coffee	25, 43
Kalifornien -s	(nn)	California	37
kamen	(v*)	→ kommen	13
Kanal -s,¨-e	(nm)	channel	43, 53
kann	(v*)	→ können	
kannst	(v*)	→ können	
Kappe -,-n	(nf)	cap	51
kaputt	(adj)	broken; broken(-down)	21; 61
Karma -s	(nn)	karma	49
Karotte -,-n	(nf)	carrot	43
Karriere -,-n	(nf)	career	57
Kartoffel -,-n	(nf)	potato	35, 43
Käse -s,-	(nm)	cheese	43
Kassette -,-n	(nf)	cassette, tape	17, 21, 45
katholisch	(adj)	Catholic	67
kaufen	(v)	to buy	19, 33
Kaufhaus -es,¨-er	(nn)	department store	21
Kaution -,-en	(nf)	deposit	19
kein	(adj)	no	21
Kellner -s,-/Kellnerin -,-nen	(nm/f)	waiter/waitress	55
kennen	(v*)	to know	17, 23, 61
kennen lernen	(v)	to get to know	29
kennst	(v*)	→ kennen	17, 61
Kind -(e)s,-er	(nn)	child	15, 31, 37, 57, 61
Kindergarten -s,¨-	(nm)	nursery school	15
Kindersendung -,-en	(nf)	children's programme	53
Kino -s,-s	(nn)	cinema	9, 21, 27, 45
Kirche -,-n	(nf)	church	67
Kirsche -,-n	(nf)	cherry	43
Klappentext -es,-e	(nm)	blurb	65
klasse	(adj)	great, super	25, 29, 37, 65
Klasse -,-n	(nf)	class	15
Klassenarbeit -,-en	(nf)	(class) test	17
Klassenzimmer -s,-	(nn)	classroom	15
klassisch	(adj)	classical	53
Kleid -(e)s,-er	(nn)	dress	51
klein	(adj)	little	31, 35, 45, 53
Kleinigkeit -,-en	(nf)	small gift, present	31

Klempner -s,-	(nm)	plumber	55
Kleopatra -	(nf)	Cleopatra	67
klicken	(v)	to click	39
klingeln	(v)	to ring	11
Klo -s,-s	(nn)	loo	19
knauserig	(adj)	stingy	31
Kneipe -,-n	(nf)	pub	13, 29
Knie -s,-	(nn)	knee	57
Knoblauch -(e)s	(nm)	garlic	43
Knöchel -s,-	(nm)	ankle	57
knutschen, sich ©	(v)	to kiss, to smooch	19
kochen	(v)	to boil	35
Kochtopf -(e)s,¨-e	(nm)	saucepan	13
Kohl -(e)s	(nm)	cabbage	43
komme mit	(v*)	→ mitkommen	39
kommen	(v*)	to come	
kommst zurecht	(v*)	→ zurechtkommen	63
Kommunikation -	(nf)	communication	23
Komödie -,-n	(nf)	comedy	13
Komponist -en,-en	(nm)	composer	45
Königin -,-nen	(nf)	queen	67
Konkurrenz -	(nf)	competition	63
können	(v*)	to be able to, can	
Kontinent -(e)s,-e	(nm)	continent	47
Konto -s,-s	(nn)	account	39
Kontostand -(e)s, ¨-e	(nm)	bank balance	31
Konzert -(e)s,-e	(nn)	concert	13
Kopfschmerzen	(npl)	headache	49, 57
Kopfweh -s	(nn)	headache	49, 57
Koran -s	(nm)	Koran	67
Körper -s,-	(nm)	body	57
krank	(adj)	ill, sick	35, 49
Krankenhaus -es,¨-er	(nn)	hospital	35
Krankenpfleger -s,-	(nm)	nurse	55
Krankenschwester -,-n	(nf)	nurse	55
Krankheit -,-en	(nf)	illness, disease	49
Kreditkarte -,-n	(nf)	credit card	31
kriegen	(v)	to get	19, 41, 63
Krimi -s,-s	(nm)	thriller	53
Krise -,-n	(nf)	crisis	19
Kritik -,-en	(nf)	review	53
Küche -,-n	(nf)	kitchen	53
Kuchen -s,-	(nm)	cake	43
Kumpel -s,-	(nm)	mate, pal	29
Kunst -,¨-e	(nf)	art	45
Kunstgalerie -,-n	(nf)	art gallery	45
Künstler -s,-/Künstlerin -,-nen	(nm/f)	artist	45
Kunststopfen -s	(nn)	invisible mending	11
Kunstwerk -(e)s,-e	(nn)	work of art	45
kurz	(adj); (adv)	short; quickly	9; 47
Kurzbesuch -(e)s,-e	(nm)	short visit	29
Kusine -,-n	(nf)	cousin	17, 37
Kuss -es,¨-e	(nm)	kiss	53
küssen	(v)	to kiss	33

L

lächeln	(v)	to smile	41
lachen	(v)	to laugh	41
Ladenbesitzer -s,-/ Ladenbesitzerin -,-nen	(nm/f)	shopkeeper	55
ladet ein	(v*)	→ einladen	29
lahm	(adj)	boring, dull	21
Lammkeule -,-n	(nf)	leg of lamb	43
Landwirt -(e)s,-e/ Landwirtin -,-nen	(nm/f)	farmer	55
Langlauf -(e)s	(nm)	cross-country skiing	61
langweilen	(v)	to bore	27
langweilen, sich	(v)	to be bored	21

GLOSSARY continued

langweilig	(adj)	boring	37
lassen	(v*)	to let	35
laufen	(v*)	to be on, to be showing; to run	21
Laufen –s	(nn)	running	61
läuft	(v*)	→ laufen	21
launisch	(adj)	moody	41
läuten	(v)	to ring	11
lauter	(adj)	nothing but	67
leben	(v)	to live	15, 57
Leben –s,–	(nn)	life	
Lebensmittelvergiftung –	(nf)	food poisoning	49
Lebensweisheiten	(npl)	words of wisdom	15
leer	(adj)	empty	15
Lehrer –s,–/ Lehrerin –,–nen	(nm/f)	teacher	55
Lehrplan –(e)s,¨–e	(nm)	curriculum	15
Lehrstelle –,–n	(nf)	training place	
leicht	(adv)	easily	49, 59
Leichtathletik –	(nf)	athletics	61
lernen	(v)	to learn	15
lesen	(v*)	to read	65
letzter/letzte/letztes	(adj)	last	19
Leute	(npl)	people	11, 15, 31
Liebe –	(nf)	love	15, 41
Liebling –s,–e	(nm)	darling	31, 53
Lied –(e)s,–er	(nn)	song	17, 45
liegen	(v*)	to lie	35
liegen lassen	(v*)	to leave (behind)	53
Limonade –,–n	(nf)	lemonade	43
Lippe –,–n	(nf)	lip	57
List –,–en	(nf)	(cunning) trick	59
Literatur –,–en	(nf)	literature	45, 55, 65
lohnen, sich	(v)	to be worth it	31
los	(adv)	come on	17
löschen	(v)	to delete	39
Lösung –,–en	(nf)	solution	25
Lunge –,–n	(nf)	lung	57
lustig	(adj)	funny	9

M

machen	(v)	to do; to make	
machst	(v)	→ machen	33
mächtig	(adj)	powerful	67
Macker –s,– ©	(nm)	mate	53
Mädchen –s,–	(nn)	girl	33, 51, 55
Magen –s, –	(nm)	stomach	57
Magenschmerzen	(npl)	stomach ache	57
Mai	(nm)	May	27
Makler –s,–	(nm)	estate agent	19
Mal –(e)s,–e	(nn)	time	41
mal = einmal	(adv)	once	33
malen	(v)	to paint	21
Malerei –	(nf)	painting	45
Mami –,–s	(nf)	mummy	25
man	(pron)	one, you	
Mann –(e)s,¨–er	(nm)	man; husband	25; 45
Mantel –s,¨–	(nm)	coat	51
Mark –	(nf)	mark	
Marke –,–n	(nf)	make	19, 43
März	(nm)	March	27
Matheprüfung –,–en	(nf)	maths exam	43
Maus –,Mäuse	(nf)	mouse	39
Mechaniker –s,–/ Mechanikerin –,–nen	(nm/f)	mechanic	55
Medien	(npl)	media	23
Medikament –(e)s,–e	(nn)	medicine	35
Meer –(e)s,–e	(nn)	sea	47
Megastore –s,–s	(nm)	megastore	29

mehr	(adv)	more	43
mein	(pron)	my	27
meinen	(v)	to think	19, 45, 51
Menü –s,–s	(nn)	menu	39
mich	(pron)	me	
Miete –,–n	(nf)	rent	19
mieten	(v)	to rent	19
Mieter –s,–/Mieterin –,–nen	(nm/f)	tenant	19
Milch –	(nf)	milk	43
Million –,–en	(nf)	million	39, 65
Mineralwasser –s	(nn)	mineral water	43
mir	(pron)	(to) me	
Mist –(e)s ©	(nm)	rubbish;	21, 65
	(interj)	damn	63
mit	(prep)	with	
Miteigentümer –s,–/ Miteigentümerin –,–nen	(nm/f)	co-owner	19
miteinander	(adv)	with each other, together	33
mithören	(v sep)	to listen in	63
mitkommen	(v sep*)	to come (along) (too)	29, 39
mitnehmen	(v sep*)	to give a lift to	59
mitnimmt	(v*)	→ mitnehmen	59
mittelmäßig	(adv)	average	63
Mittwoch	(nm)	Wednesday	27
Mobiltelefon –s,–e	(nn)	mobile (phone)	23, 35
möchten	(v)	→ mögen	43
mögen	(v*)	to like	33, 43
Möhre –,–n	(nf)	carrot	43
monatlich	(adv)	monthly	63
Mond –(e)s,–e	(nm)	moon	47
Montag	(nm)	Monday	27
Moped –s,–s	(nn)	moped	59
morgen	(adv)	tomorrow	43, 45
Morgenrock –(e)s, ¨–e	(nm)	dressing gown	51
Moschee –,–n	(nf)	mosque	67
Moslem –s,–e/ Moslime –,–n	(nm/f)	Muslim	67
moslemisch	(adj)	Muslim	67
motivieren	(v)	to motivate	37
Motorrad –(e)s,¨–er	(nn)	motorcycle	59
Motorroller –s,–	(nm)	scooter	59
Mückenstich –s,–e	(nm)	mosquito bite	49
Münze –,–n	(nf)	coin	31
Museum –s,–seen	(nn)	museum	29, 45
Musik –	(nf)	music	21, 45
Musiker –s,–/Musikerin –,–nen	(nm/f)	musician	55
Musikkapelle –,–n	(nf)	band	53
muss	(v*)	→ müssen	29, 31, 55
müssen	(v*)	to have to, must	
musste, mussten	(v*)	→ müssen	13
Mutter –,¨–	(nf)	mother	
Mutti –,–s	(nf)	mum	25, 53, 59
Mütze –,–n	(nf)	cap	51

N

nach	(prep)	to	37
nachdenken	(v sep*)	to think about	55
Nachfrage –,–n	(nf)	demand	63
nachgedacht	(v*)	→ nachdenken	55
Nachname –ns,–n	(nm)	surname	9
nachrennen	(v sep*)	to chase after, to pursue	39
Nachricht –,–en	(nf)	message	23
Nachrichten	(npl)	news	23, 53
nachspionieren	(v sep)	to spy on	41
nächster/nächste/nächstes	(adj)	next; nearest, next	41; 59
Nachtclub –s,–s	(nm)	nightclub	13
nachts	(adv)	at night	41
Name –ns,–n	(nm)	name	65
Nasenkorrektur –,–en	(nf)	nose job	57

natürlich	(adv)	of course, naturally	
ne ⓖ	(adv)	no	21, 45, 53
Nebel -s,-	(nm)	fog	47
neben	(prep)	next to	17, 35
Nebenanschluss -es,¨-e	(nm)	extension number	35
nebenbei	(adv)	vaguely	53
Neffe -n,-n	(nm)	nephew	17
nehmen	(v*)	to take	59
nein	(adv)	no	
nett	(adj)	pleasant;	9;
		nice	31
Netz -es,-e	(nn)	Internet, Net	39
neu	(adj)	new	21, 47
neun	(number)	nine	61, 65
neunter/neunte/neuntes	(adj)	ninth	61
neunundzwanzig	(number)	twenty-nine	65
neunzehn	(number)	nineteen	65
neunzig	(number)	ninety	65
nicht	(adv)	not	
Nichte -,-n	(nf)	niece	17
nichts	(pron)	nothing	23, 27
nie	(adv)	never	27
niemand	(pron)	nobody	9, 67
noch	(adv)	still	33
Notar -s,-e	(nm)	notary	55
Notarzt -es,¨-e	(nm)	(emergency) doctor	13
Note -,-n	(nf)	mark, grade;	15, 47;
		note	53
Notfall -(e)s,¨-e	(nm)	emergency	59
November	(nm)	November	27
Nudeln	(nf pl)	pasta	43
null	(number)	zero	65
Nummer -,-n	(nf)	number	11
nur	(adv)	only	21, 33

O

ob	(conj)	whether, if	21
Oberschenkel -s,-	(nm)	thigh	57
Oberstufe -,-n	(nf)	sixth form	15
obwohl	(conj)	although	27
oder	(conj)	or	
öffentlich	(adj)	public	63
oh	(interj)	oh	11, 31
ohne	(prep)	without	61
Ohr -(e)s,-en	(nn)	ear	57
Ohrenschmerzen	(npl)	earache	49
okay	(adv)	OK	29, 33, 43, 59
Oktober	(nm)	October	27
Öl -(e)s,-e	(nn)	oil	43
Olympiade -,-n	(nf)	Olympics, Olympic Games	61
Oma -,-s	(nf)	granny	53
Onkel -s,-	(nm)	uncle	17, 19
Oper -,-n	(nf)	opera;	13, 45;
		opera house	13
operieren	(v)	to operate (on)	49, 57
Orange -,-n	(nf)	orange	43
orthodox	(adj)	Orthodox	67
Osterferien	(npl)	Easter holiday/vacation	37
Ozean -s,-e	(nm)	ocean	47

P

paar, ein	(pron)	a few	
Paket -(e)s,-e	(nn)	parcel	23
Palast -(e)s,¨-e	(nm)	palace	49
Paprikaschote -,-n	(nf)	pepper	43
Papst -(e)s,¨-e	(nm)	pope	67
Park -s,-s	(nm)	park	27
Party -,-s	(nf)	party	13

Passwort -(e)s,¨-er	(nn)	password	39
Pause -,-n	(nf)	break	45
PC -(s),-(s)	(nm)	computer, PC	39
Penizillin -s	(nn)	penicillin	49
Pension -,-en	(nf)	guest house	29
Pferdeschwanz -es,¨-e	(nm)	pony-tail	9
Pfirsich -s,-e	(nm)	peach	43
Pflaume -,-n	(nf)	plum	43
Pfund -(e)s	(nn)	pound	31
Pickel -s,-	(nm)	spot, pimple	49
Piepser -s,-	(nm)	pager	23
Pilot -en,-en/Pilotin -,-nen	(nm/f)	pilot	55
Pizza -,-s	(nf)	pizza	43
Plan -(e)s,¨-e	(nm)	plan	29, 37
plane ein	(v)	→ einplanen	57
Plastik -,-en	(nf)	sculpture	45
Platte -,-n	(nf)	record	21
Plattenladen -s,¨-	(nm)	music shop	21
Platz -es,¨-e	(nm)	seat	59
Pleite -,-n ⓖ	(nf)	flop	13
Pokerspiel -s,-e	(nn)	game of poker	59
Post -	(nf)	post office	23
Postbote -n,-n/Postbotin -,-nen	(nm/f)	postman/postwoman	55
Postfach -(e)s,¨-er	(nn)	PO box	23
postlagernd	(adv)	post-restante	23
Predigt -,-en	(nf)	sermon	67
Preis -es,-e	(nm)	price	19, 31, 63
Presse -	(nf)	press	23
Priester -s,-	(nm)	priest	67
prima	(adj)	great	25
Prinz -en,-en	(nm)	prince	67
Prise -,-n	(nf)	pinch	35
Privatwirtschaft -	(nf)	private sector	63
pro	(prep)	per	19
Problem -s,-e	(nn)	problem	55
Programm -s,-e	(nn)	listing, entertainment	
		guide	13
programmieren	(v)	to program	21
Programmierer -s,-/			
Programmiererin -,-nen	(nm/f)	programmer	55
protestantisch	(adj)	Protestant	67
Prüfung -,-en	(nf)	exam, examination	13, 15
Pullover -s,-	(nm)	sweater	51
Putzfrau -,-en	(nf)	cleaner, charwoman	49

Q

Quadratmeter -s,-	(nm)	square metre	19
Quatsch -(e)s ⓖ	(nm)	rubbish	39, 49

R

Rad -(e)s,¨-er	(nn)	bicycle	59
Radfahren -s	(nn)	cycling	61
Radio -s,-s	(nn)	radio	23
Ranch -, -(e)s	(nf)	ranch	29
raten	(v*)	to guess	19
rausschmeißen ⓖ	(v sep*)	to chuck, ditch	55
Realschule -,-n	(nf)	secondary school	15
Recht -(e)s,-e	(nn)	right	67
Rechtsanwalt -(e)s,¨-e	(nm)	lawyer	61
reden	(v)	to talk	29, 63
Regenmantel -s,¨-	(nm)	raincoat	51
Regenwald -(e)s,¨-er	(nm)	rainforest	47
Regisseur -s,-e	(nm)	director	45
reinkriegen ⓖ	(v sep)	to get	43
Reis -es	(nm)	rice	43
Reise -,-n	(nf)	journey	29, 59
reist herum	(v)	→ herumreisen	15
Reiten -s	(nn)	horse riding	61

reparieren	(v)	to repair	61
reservieren	(v)	to book	29
Ressource -,-n	(nf)	resource	47
Rezeption -	(nf)	reception desk	29
richtig	(adj);	right, correct;	25;
	(adv)	properly	29
Riesendachterrassenwohnung -,-en	(nf)	huge roof-terrace flat	61
Rinderbraten -s,-	(nm)	roast beef	43
Rock -(e)s,-̈e	(nm)	skirt	51
Rollkragenpulli -s,-s	(nm)	polo neck	51
Rollschuhlaufen -s	(nn)	roller skating	61
romantisch	(adj)	romantic	65
Rosenkohl -(e)s	(nm)	Brussels sprouts	43
rot	(adj)	red	57
Rückweg -(e)s,-e	(nm)	way back	59
ruf zurück	(v*)	→ zurückrufen	29
rufe ab	(v*)	→ abrufen	39
rufen	(v*)	to call	13
rufst an	(v*)	→ anrufen	39
Rugby -(s)	(nn)	rugby	61
Ruhe -	(nf)	silence	53
ruhig	(adj)	quiet	17
Rundreise -,-n	(nf)	tour	29
runterfahren ⊚	(v sep*)	to go down	61
runterrasen ⊚	(v sep)	to rush down	61

S

S-Bahn -,-en	(nf)	local train, city and suburban railway	59
sagen	(v)	to say; to tell	
Salami -,-s	(nf)	salami	43
Salat -(e)s,-e	(nm)	lettuce	43
Salz -es,-e	(nn)	salt	35, 43
Samstag	(nm)	Saturday	27
Satellitenschüssel -,-n	(nf)	satellite dish	43
Saum -s,-̈e	(nm)	hem	11
Schach -s	(nn)	chess	21
schaffen	(v)	to manage	45
schälen	(v)	to peel	35
Schatz -es,-̈e	(nm)	darling	27
Schauspieler -s,-/Schauspielerin -,-nen	(nm/f)	actor/actress	9, 55
Scheck -s,-s	(nm)	cheque	31
Scheckbuch -(e)s,-̈er	(nn)	cheque book	31
Scheckkarte -,-n	(nf)	cheque card, cash card	31
scheiden lassen, sich	(v)	to divorce	17
schenken	(v)	to give (as a present)	31, 45
schicken	(v)	to send	35, 37, 39, 45
Schicksal -s, -e	(nn)	destiny, fate	49
Schiff -(e)s,-e	(nn)	boat	59
schlafen	(v*)	to sleep	41
Schlafzimmer -s,-	(nn)	bedroom	19
Schlägerei -,-en	(nf)	fight, punch-up	13
Schlagzeuger -s,-	(nm)	drummer	9
schlank	(adj)	slim	9
schlecht	(adj)	bad	65
schließlich	(adv)	finally; after all	13; 67
Schlosserei -,-en	(nf)	locksmith	11
Schlüpfer -s,-	(nm)	knickers	51
schmeißen ⊚	(v*)	to chuck	13
Schnappschuss -es,-̈e	(nm)	snapshot	51
Schnee -s	(nm)	snow	47
schnell	(adv)	quickly	13
Schnitt -(e)s	(nm)	cutting	45
Schnupfen -s	(nm)	cold	49
schnurlos	(adj)	cordless	35
Schnurrbart -(e)s,-̈e	(nm)	moustache	9
schon	(adv)	already; yet	27, 31, 41; 33

Schönheitssalon -s,-s	(nm)	beauty salon	11
schreiben	(v*)	to write	23, 45, 47
Schriftsteller -s,-/ Schriftstellerin -,-nen	(nm/f)	author	45
Schuh -(e)s,-e	(nm)	shoe	51
Schule -,-n	(nf)	school	19
Schüler -s,-/Schülerin -,-nen	(nm/f)	pupil	15
Schulferien	(npl)	school holidays/vacation	37
Schulter -,-n	(nf)	shoulder	57
Schwager -s,-	(nm)	brother-in-law	17
Schwägerin -,-nen	(nf)	sister-in-law	17
schwanger	(adj)	pregnant	49
Schweinefleisch -(e)s	(nn)	pork	43
Schwester -,-n	(nf)	sister	17, 35
Schwiegermutter -,-̈	(nf)	mother-in-law	17
Schwiegersohn -(e)s,-̈e	(nm)	son-in-law	17
Schwiegertochter -,-̈	(nf)	daughter-in-law	17
Schwiegervater -s,-̈	(nm)	father-in-law	17
schwimmen	(v*)	to swim	21, 61
Schwimmen	(nn)	swimming	61
schwindlig	(adj)	dizzy	49
sechs	(number)	six	65
Sechs -,-en	(nf)	six	47
sechsstellig	(adj)	six-figure	39
sechsundzwanzig	(number)	twenty-six	65
sechzehn	(number)	sixteen	65
sechzig	(number)	sixty	65
See -,-n	(nf)	sea	47
See -s,-n	(nm)	lake	59
seh aus	(v*)	→ aussehen	51
sehen	(v*)	to see; to watch	19, 27, 35; 53
sehr	(adv)	very	
Seifenoper -,-n	(nf)	soap opera	53
sein	(v*);	to be;	27;
	(adj)	his	13
seit	(conj)	since	27
seitdem	(adv)	since	27
selbst	(adv);	even;	33;
	(pron)	herself	61
Selbstmord -(e)s,-e	(nm)	suicide	13
selten	(adj)	rare	27
Sendung -,-en	(nf)	programme	53
September	(nm)	September	27
setzt ab	(v)	→ absetzen	59
setzt sich hin	(v)	→ hinsetzen, sich	63
Shopping -s	(nn)	shopping	29
Show -,-s	(nf)	show	13
sicherlich	(adv)	surely	45
sichern	(v)	to back up	39
sie	(pron)	she; they; them; you	
Sie	(pron)	you	
sieben	(number)	seven	65
siebenundzwanzig	(number)	twenty-seven	65
siebzehn	(number)	seventeen	65
siebzig	(number)	seventy	65
sind	(v*)	→ sein	
sinfonisch	(adj)	symphonic	53
sitz/sitzt	(v*)	→ sitzen	17
sitzen	(v*)	to sit	17
Skiurlaub -(e)s,-e	(nm)	skiing holidays/vacation	37
Skiurlaubsort -(e)s,-e	(nm)	ski resort	47
sklavisch	(adv)	slavishly	39
Skulptur -	(nf)	sculpture	45
Snowboarden -s	(nn)	snowboarding	37
so	(adv)	so;	17, 23;

so		like this, like that;	39;
		such	39, 49
sobald	(conj)	as soon as	61
sofort	(adv)	at once, immediately	49
Softie –s,–s	(nm)	wimp	33
sogar	(adv)	even	25
Sohn –(e)s,¨-e	(nm)	son	17, 27, 31
solcher/solche/solches	(adj)	such	37
sollen	(v*)	should	23
Sommerferien	(npl)	summer holidays/vacation	37
Sonnabend –s	(nm)	Sunday	27
Sonne –,–n	(nf)	sun	47
Sonntag –s	(nm)	Sunday	27, 37
sonst	(adv)	otherwise, or (else)	41
Sorge –,–n	(nf)	worry	41
sowieso	(adv)	anyway	31, 39, 55
Spaß –es,¨-e	(nm)	fun	13, 15, 59
später	(adv)	later	29
speichern	(v)	to save	39
Spiegelbild –(e)s,–er	(nn)	reflection	65
spielen	(v)	to play	21, 53, 61
Spielfilm –(e)s,–e	(nm)	film	53
Spielhalle –,–n	(nf)	amusement arcade	13
Spielplatz –es,¨-e	(nm)	playground	61
spinnen Ⓡ	(v)	to be nuts	33
Spitzname –ns,–n	(nm)	nickname	9
sponsern	(v)	to sponsor	35
Sport –(e)s	(nm)	sport	61
sportlich	(adj)	athletic	61
Sportsendung –,–en	(nf)	sport	53
sprechen	(v*)	to talk, to speak	9, 23
spricht	(v*)	→ sprechen	9
Squash –	(nn)	squash	21
Staaten, die	(npl)	the States	29
staatlich	(adj)	public	63
Stadtzentrum –s, –tren	(nn)	city centre	19
Stammbaum –(e)s,¨-e	(nm)	family tree	45
ständig	(adj);	constant;	15;
	(adv)	constantly;	23;
		all the time	19
stark	(adj)	fantastic, brilliant	25
stecken	(v)	to put	23
stehlen	(v*)	to steal	35
steht auf	(v*)	→ aufstehen	63
Stellung –,–en	(nf)	job	31
sterben	(v*)	to die	15
Stern –(e)s,–e	(nm)	star	47
Steuer –,–n	(nf)	tax	65
Steuergruppe –,–n	(nf)	tax bracket	63
Stich –(e)s,–e	(nm)	engraving	45
Stiefbruder –s,¨-	(nm)	stepbrother	17, 23, 45
Stiefel –s,-	(nm)	boot	51
Stiefmutter –,¨-	(nf)	stepmother	17
Stiefschwester –,–n	(nf)	stepsister	17
Stiefvater –s,¨-	(nm)	stepfather	17, 23
stinken	(v*)	to smell	17
stinklangweilig	(adj)	deadly boring	33
stinkst	(v*)	→ stinken	17
stirbt	(v*)	→ sterben	15
Stock –(e)s	(nm)	floor	61
stören	(v)	to disturb	35
Straße –,–n	(nf)	street	41
Straßenbahn –,–en	(nf)	tram	59
Strumpfhose –,–n	(nf)	(pair of) tights	51
Student –en,–en/Studentin –,–nen	(nm/f)	student	15
Studio –s,–s	(nn)	studio	29
Studium –s,–ien	(nn)	studies	55
Stunde –,–n	(nf)	hour	23, 61
Subvention –,–en	(nf)	subsidy	63
suchen	(v)	to search	39

Suchmaschine –,–n	(nf)	search engine	39
Sultan –s,–e	(nm)	sultan	67
Suppe –,–n	(nf)	soup	43
surfen	(v)	to surf	21
süß	(adj)	sweet, cute	15
sympathisch	(adj)	nice	9

T

T-Shirt –s,–s	(nn)	T-shirt	51
Tag –(e)s,–e	(nm)	day	29
Tagesmutter –,¨-	(nf)	childminder	17
Tageszeitung –,–en	(nf)	daily paper	23
Taille –,–n	(nf)	waist	57
Takt –(e)s	(nm)	tact, tactfulness	33
Talkshow –,–s	(nf)	talk show	53
Tankwart –(e)s,¨-e/Tankwärtin –,–nen	(nm/f)	petrol-pump attendant	55
Tante –,–n	(nf)	aunt	17, 31
Tanz –es,¨-e	(nm)	dance	45
Taschenbuch –(e)s,¨-er	(nn)	paperback	45
Taschengeld –(e)s,–er	(rin)	pocket money	63
Tastatur –,–en	(nf)	keyboard	39
tausend	(number)	thousand	65
Taxi –s,–s	(nn)	taxi, cab	41, 43, 59
Techniker –s,-/Technikerin –,–nen	(nm/f)	engineer	55
Tee –s	(nm)	tea	43
Telefax –,–(e)	(nn)	fax (machine/ message)	23
Telefon –s,–e	(nn)	(tele)phone	11, 23, 39
Telefonbuch –(e)s,¨-er	(nn)	phone book	35
Telefonkarte –,–n	(nf)	phone card	23, 35
Telefonnummer –,–n	(nf)	(tele)phone number	23, 33
Telefonzelle –,–n	(nf)	phone box	23
Telekommunikation –	(nf)	telecommunications	23
Tennis –	(nn)	tennis	21, 61
Teppich –s, –e	(nm)	carpet, rug	13
Text –(e)s,–e	(nm)	lyrics, words	17
Theater –s,-	(nn)	theatre	13, 45
Theaterstück	(nn)	play	13
Thema –s,–men	(nn)	subject	15
Tierarzt –es,¨-e/ Tierärztin –,–nen	(nm/f)	vet	55
tja	(int)	(yes) well	37
Tochter –,¨-	(nf)	daughter	17
Toilette –,–n	(nf)	toilet	19, 65
toll	(adj)	great;	9
		brilliant	37
Ton –(e)s,¨-e	(nm)	note	53
Top –s,–s	(nn)	top	51
Topf –(e)s,¨-e	(nm)	saucepan	35
Tourismus –	(nm)	tourism	63
trampen Ⓡ	(v)	to hitch-hike	41
Tränengasbombe –,–n	(nf)	tear-gas canister	13
Traum –(e)s,¨-e	(nm)	dream	29
Träumerei –,–en	(nf)	day dream	39
Traumfrau –,–en	(nf)	dream woman	57
Traurigkeit –	(nf)	sadness	41
Treff –s,–s	(nm)	get-together, meeting-place	13
treffen	(v*)	to meet;	15;
		to hit (on)	25
Treffpunkt –(e)s,–e	(nm)	meeting-place	35
treiben	(v*)	to do	61
Treppe –,–n	(nf)	stairs	61
Treppensteigen –s	(nn)	climbing stairs	61
triffst	(v*)	→ treffen	15
trinken	(v*)	to drink	43
tropisch	(adj)	tropical	47
tschüss!	(interj)	bye! see you!	11
Typ –en or–s,–en	(nm)	bloke, guy	33

U

U-Bahn -,-en	(nf)	underground, tube	59
U-Bahn-Station -,-en	(nf)	underground station	59
über	(prep)	about	17
überfallen	(v*)	to mug	41
übergeben, sich	(v)	to be sick	49
überhaupt	(adv)	at all	29
überhaupt nicht	(adv)	not at all	51
überlegen, sich	(v)	to think (about)	45
übertreiben	(v*)	to go over the top	61
überweisen	(v*)	to transfer	39
um	(conj)	(in order) to	13
umgekehrt	(adv)	the other way round	49
umsteigen	(v sep*)	to change	59
umstoßen	(v sep*)	to knock over	13
umtauschen	(v sep)	to change	31
und	(conj)	and	
ungefähr	(adv)	about, approximately	19
ungerecht	(adj)	unfair	47
ungewöhnlich	(adj)	unusual	65
unglaublich	(adj)	incredible, unbelievable	19, 65
Universität -,-en	(nf)	university	15
unlesbar	(adj)	unreadable	65
unmöglich	(adj)	impossible	39, 41
uns	(pron)	us	
unser	(adj)	our	
unten	(adv)	downstairs	61
Unterhaltung -	(nf)	entertainment	13
Unterhose -,-n	(nf)	underpants	51
Unternehmen -s,-	(nn)	company	63
Unterricht -s,-e	(nm)	lessons	35
Untertitel -s,-	(nm)	subtitle	45
Unterwäsche -	(nf)	underwear	51
ununterbrochen	(adv)	constantly	11

V

Vater -s,-¨-	(nm)	father	
Vati -s,-s	(nm)	dad	31
Verbrauch -(e)s	(nm)	consumption	63
Verbraucher -s,-/ Verbraucherin -,-nen	(nm/f)	consumer	63
verdienen	(v)	to earn	31, 55
vereinbaren	(v)	to arrange	59
verfluchen	(v)	to curse	49
vergessen	(v*)	to forget	17, 43
Vergnügen, -s	(nn)	pleasure	41
Vergnügungspark -s,-s	(nm)	theme park	13
verheiratet	(adj)	married	17
verkaufen, sich	(v)	to sell	65
Verkaufspreis -es,-e	(nm)	retail price	63
verknallt ◎	(adj)	in love	33
verlangen	(v)	to ask	11
verletzen	(v)	to hurt	41
verlieben, sich	(v)	to fall in love	15
vermieten	(v)	to let	19
Verschlüsselung -,-en	(nf)	coding, code	39
verstanden	(v*)	→ verstehen	41
verständigen	(v)	to notify, inform	23
verständigen, sich	(v)	to communicate	23
verstehen	(v*)	to understand	25, 33, 39, 41
versuchen	(v)	to try	23
verwählen, sich	(v)	to misdial, dial the wrong number	11
Verwandte -n,-n	(nm/f)	relation	17
verwechseln	(v)	to mix up	27
Vetter -s,-n	(nm)	cousin	17, 37
Video -s,-s	(nn)	video (cassette)	21, 43
Videokamera -,-s	(nf)	video camera	45
Videorekorder -s,-	(nm)	video recorder	21

viel	(pron)	a lot	15
Vielfraß -es,-¨-e ◎	(nm)	greedy-guts, greedy pig	13
vielleicht	(adv)	perhaps	21, 45
vier	(number)	four	65
Viertelstunde -,-n	(nf)	quarter of an hour	35
vierundzwanzig	(number)	twenty-four	65
vierzehn	(number)	fourteen	65
vierzig	(number)	forty	65
Voice-Mail -s	(nf)	voice mail	35
Volk -(e)s,-¨-er	(nn)	people	67
völlig	(adj);	complete;	13;
	(adv)	completely, totally	17
Vollpension -	(nf)	full board	29
von	(prep)	of; from	
vorhaben	(v sep*)	to intend	37
Vorort -(e)s,-e	(nm)	suburb	19
Vorschlag -(e)s,-¨-e	(nm)	proposal	25
Vorschule -,-n	(nf)	nursery school	15
vorstellen, sich	(v sep*)	to imagine	53
Vorwahl -,-en	(nf)	code	35

W

Wachstum -s	(nn)	growth	63
Wagen -s,-	(nm)	car	59
wählen	(v)	to dial	11, 35
wahnsinnig	(adv)	terribly	31
wann	(adv)	when	17, 33
war, warst, wart	(v*)	→ sein	67
warten	(v)	to wait	63
warum	(adv)	why	
was	(pron)	what	37
Wasser -s	(nn)	water	13, 35, 43
Wasserskilaufen -s	(nn)	water skiing	61
Web-Site -,-s	(nf)	web site	23
Wechselgeld -(e)s	(nn)	small change	31
wechseln	(v)	to change	31
wecken	(v)	to wake (up)	41
weg	(adv)	gone	27
wegfressen ◎	(v sep*)	to eat up all the food	13
weggehen	(v sep*)	to go out	13, 33, 41
wegsaufen ◎	(v sep*)	to drink up all the drink	13
weigern, sich	(v)	to refuse	25
Weihnachtsferien	(npl)	Christmas holiday/ vacation	37
weil	(conj)	because	
Wein -s,-e	(nm)	wine	43
weinen	(v)	to cry	13, 41
Weintraube -,-n	(nf)	grape	43
weiß, weißt	(v*)	→ wissen	41
weit	(adv)	far	21
welcher/welche/welches	(pron)	which	19, 25, 43
Welt -,-en	(nf)	world	15
wen	(pron)	who, whom	11
wenn	(conj)	if; when	
wer	(pron)	who	9
Werbung -	(nf)	adverts	53
werden	(v*)	to become	49
wesentlich	(adv)	much, considerably	39
Wetter -s	(nn)	weather	47
Wetterbericht -(e)s, -e	(nm)	weather forecast	53
wichtig	(adj)	important	11
Wichtigste -n	(nn)	the most important thing	39
wie	(conj);	like, as;	27, 31;
	(adv)	how	19, 65
wieder	(adv)	again	27, 63
Wiedergeburt -,-en	(nf)	reincarnation	67

wiederholen	(v)	to repeat	35
wiegen	(v*)	to weigh	9
Wiener Würstchen	(nn pl)	sausages	43
wild ⊚	(adj)	mad	55
will	(v*)	→ **wollen**	41, 45, 63
willst	(v*)	→ **wollen**	55
wir	(pron)	we	21
wird	(v*)	→ **werden**	31
wirklich	(adv)	really	
Wirtschaftslage –	(nf)	economic situation	63
wissen	(v*)	to know	
witzig	(adj)	funny	37
wo	(adv)	where	
Woche –,–n	(nf)	week	29
Wohnblock –(e)s,–s	(nm)	block of flats	19
wohnen	(v)	to live	49
Wohngemeinschaft –,–en	(nf)	group sharing a flat or house	19
Wohnung –,–en	(nf)	flat	13, 19
Wohnzimmer –s,–	(nn)	sitting room	19
wollen	(v*)	to want	63
wusstest	(v*)	→ **wissen**	19

Y

Yoga –(s)	(nn)	yoga	21

Z

zahlen	(v)	to pay	19, 43, 65
Zahlenkombinaton –,–en	(nf)	(number) code	23
Zahlungsbilanz –,–en	(nf)	balance of payments	35, 63
Zahnarzt –es,¨–e/ Zahnärztin –,–nen	(nm/f)	dentist	55
Zahnschmerzen	(npl)	toothache	49
Zeh –s,–en	(nm)	toe	57
zehn	(number)	ten	65
Zeichen –s,–	(nn)	sign, signal	9
Zeichnung –,–en	(nf)	drawing	45
Zeitschrift –,–en	(nf)	magazine	13, 23
zentnerschwer	(adj)	weighing a ton, that weighs a ton	61
Zentralasien –s	(nn)	Central Asia	47
zerstören	(v)	to destroy	15
Zettel –s,–	(nm)	note	35
Zeug –s	(nn)	clothes, stuff	51
Zeugnis –ses,–se	(nn)	report	15
Zimmer –s,–	(nn)	room	49
Zitrone	(nf)	lemon	43
zu	(prep); (adv)	to; too	23, 37; 21
Zubehör –s	(nn)	equipment	45
Zucker –s	(nm)	sugar	43
zuckerkrank	(adj)	diabetic	49
zufällig	(adv)	by chance	39
Zug –(e)s,¨–e	(nm)	train	59
Zugang –(e)s,¨–e	(nm)	access	39
zugegeben	(adv)	admittedly	33
zuhören	(v sep)	to listen	9, 29, 35
Zukunft –	(nf)	future	15
zukünftig	(adj)	future	49
Zukunftsplan –(e)s,¨–e	(nm)	future plan, plan for the future	55
zuletzt	(adv)	last	27
zunehmen	(v sep*)	to put on weight	57
zurechtkommen	(v sep*)	to get on	63
zurück	(adv)	back	59
zurückbringen	(v sep*)	to bring back	27
zurückfahren	(v sep*)	to drive back	59
zurückfährt	(v*)	→ **zurückfahren**	59
zurückkam	(v*)	→ **zurückkommen**	61

zurückkommen	(v sep*)	to come back	61
zurückrufen	(v sep*)	to call back	29
zusammen	(adv)	together	19, 33
Zusammenhang –s,¨–e	(nm)	context	25
zusammenleben	(v sep)	to live together	17
Zustand –(e)s,¨–e	(nm)	state	15
Zustimmung –,–en	(nf)	approval	25
zwanzig	(number)	twenty	65
zwar	(adv)	admittedly	33
zwei	(number)	two	43, 65
zweitens	(adv)	secondly	33
zweiter/zweite/zweites	(adj)	second	47
zweiundzwanzig	(number)	twenty-two	65
Zwiebel –,–n	(nf)	onion	43
Zwillinge	(nm pl)	twins	17
zwischen	(prep)	between	45, 57
zwölf	(number)	twelve	65

VERBS

Irregular verbs

Infinitive	Present	Imperfect	Perfect
	ich, du, er/sie/es	er/sie/es	er/sie/es
abnehmen → nehmen			
abrufen → rufen			
abschreiben → schreiben			
anfangen → fangen			
angehen → gehen			
anhaben → haben			
anrufen → rufen			
anziehen → ziehen			
aufgeben → geben			
aufnehmen → nehmen			
aufstehen → stehen			
ausgehen → gehen			
aussehen → sehen			
aussprechen → sprechen			
beißen	beiße, beißt, beißt	biss	hat gebissen
bekommen	bekomme, bekommst, bekommt	bekam	hat bekommen
bestehen → stehen			
bitten	bitte, bittest, bittet	bat	hat gebeten
bleiben	bleibe, bleibst, bleibt	blieb	ist geblieben
bringen	bringe, bringst, bringt	brachte	hat gebracht
denken	denke, denkst, denkt	dachte	hat gedacht
durchfallen → fallen			
durchkommen → kommen			
dürfen	darf, darfst, darf	durfte	hat gedurft
eingeben → geben			
einladen	lade ein, lädst ein, lädt ein	lud ein	hat eingeladen
einschließen → schließen			
einwerfen → werfen			
entscheiden	entscheide, entscheidest, entscheidet	entschied	hat entschieden
entwachsen → wachsen			
erhalten → halten			
essen	esse, isst, isst	aß	hat gegessen
fahren	fahre, fährst, fährt	fuhr	ist gefahren
fallen	falle, fällst, fällt	fiel	ist gefallen
fangen	fange, fängst, fängt	fing	hat gefangen
fernsehen → sehen			
festnehmen → nehmen			
feststehen → stehen			
finden	finde, findest, findet	fand	hat gefunden
fliegen	fliege, fliegst, fliegt	flog	ist geflogen
fressen	fresse, frisst, frisst	fraß	hat gefressen
geben	gebe, gibst, gibt	gab	hat gegeben
gehen	gehe, gehst, geht	ging	ist gegangen
genießen	genieße, genießt, genießt	genoss	hat genossen
gießen	gieße, gießt, gießt	goss	hat gegossen
haben	habe, hast, hat	hatte	hat gehabt
halten	halte, hältst, hält	hielt	hat gehalten
heißen	heiße, heißt, heißt	hieß	hat geheißen
helfen	helfe, hilfst, hilft	half	hat geholfen
hinfahren → fahren			
hingehen → gehen			
hinweisen	weise hin, weist hin, weist hin	wies hin	hat hingewiesen
hochgehen → gehen			
kennen	kenne, kennst, kennt	kannte	hat gekannt
kommen	komme, kommst, kommt	kam	ist gekommen
können	kann, kannst, kann	konnte	hat gekonnt
lassen	lasse, lässt, lässt	ließ	hat gelassen
laufen	laufe, läufst, läuft	lief	ist gelaufen
lesen	lese, liest, liest	las	hat gelesen
liegen	liege, liegst, liegt	lag	hat gelegen
mitkommen → kommen			
mitnehmen → nehmen			
mögen	mag, magst, mag	mochte	hat gemocht
müssen	muss, musst, muss	musste	hat gemusst
nachdenken → denken			
nachrennen → rennen			
nehmen	nehme, nimmst, nimmt	nahm	hat genommen
nennen	nenne, nennst, nennt	nannte	hat genannt
raten	rate, rätst, rät	riet	hat geraten

Infinitive	Present	Imperfect	Perfect
rausschmeißen → schmeißen			
rennen	renne, rennst, rennt	rannte	ist gerannt
rufen	rufe, rufst, ruft	rief	hat gerufen
runterfahren → fahren			
saufen	saufe, säufst, säuft	soff	hat gesoffen
schlafen	schlafe, schläfst, schläft	schlief	hat geschlafen
schließen	schließe, schließt, schließt	schloss	hat geschlossen
schmeißen	schmeiße, schmeißt, schmeißt	schmiss	hat geschmissen
schreiben	schreibe, schreibst, schreibt	schrieb	hat geschrieben
schreien	schreie, schreist, schreit	schrie	hat geschrien
schwimmen	schwimme, schwimmst, schwimmt	schwamm	ist geschwommen
sehen	sehe, siehst, sieht	sah	hat gesehen
sein	bin, bist, ist	war	ist gewesen
singen	singe, singst, singt	sang	hat gesungen
sitzen	sitze, sitzt, sitzt	saß	hat gesessen
sollen	soll, sollst, soll	sollte	hat gesollt
sprechen	spreche, sprichst, spricht	sprach	hat gesprochen
stehen	stehe, stehst, steht	stand	hat gestanden
stehlen	stehle, stiehlst, stiehlt	stahl	hat gestohlen
steigen	steige, steigst, steigt	stieg	ist gestiegen
sterben	sterbe, stirbst, stirbt	starb	ist gestorben
stinken	stinke, stinkst, stinkt	stank	hat gestunken
stoßen	stoße, stößt, stößt	stieß	hat gestoßen
treffen	treffe, triffst, trifft	traf	hat getroffen
treiben	treibe, treibst, treibt	trieb	hat getrieben
trinken	trinke, trinkst, trinkt	trank	hat getrunken
tun	tue, tust, tut	tat	hat getan
überfallen → fallen			
übertreiben → treiben			
überweisen	überweise, überweist, überweist	überwies	hat überwiesen
umsteigen → steigen			
umstoßen → stoßen			
vergessen	vergesse, vergisst, vergisst	vergaß	hat vergessen
verlieren	verliere, verlierst, verliert	verlor	hat verloren
verstehen	verstehe, verstehst, versteht	verstand	hat verstanden
vorhaben → haben			
wachsen	wachse, wächst, wächst	wuchs	ist gewachsen
wegfressen → fressen			
weggehen → gehen			
wegsaufen → saufen			
werden	werde, wirst, wird	wurde	ist geworden
werfen	werfe, wirfst, wirft	warf	hat geworfen
wiegen	wiege, wiegst, wiegt	wog	hat gewogen
wissen	weiß, weißt, weiß	wusste	hat gewusst
wollen	will, willst, will	wollte	hat gewollt
ziehen	ziehe, ziehst, zieht	zog	hat gezogen
zunehmen → nehmen			
zurechtkommen → kommen			
zurückbringen → bringen			
zurückfahren → fahren			
zurückkommen → kommen			
zurückrufen → rufen